What's the Stor

Anne Bogart is an award-winning theater maker and a bestselling writer of books about theater, art and cultural politics. In this, her latest collection of essays, she explores the storytelling impulse and asks how she, as a "product of postmodernism," can reconnect to the primal act of making meaning and telling stories. She also asks how theater practitioners can think of themselves not as stagers of plays but as "orchestrators of social interactions" and participants in an ongoing dialogue about the future.

> We dream. And then occasionally we attempt to share our dreams with others. In recounting our dreams we impose narratives upon the barrage of images and notions that our dreams produce. We also make stories out of the blips and bleeps of our daytime existence. The human brain is a narrative-creating machine that takes whatever happens and imposes chronology, meaning, cause and effect ... We choose. We can choose to relate to our circumstances with bitterness or with openness. The stories that we tell determine nothing less than personal destiny.

This compelling new book is characteristically made up of chapters with one-word titles: Narrative, Heat, Error, Limits, Opposition, Arrest, Spaciousness, Empathy, Collaboration, Politics and Sustenance. In addition to dipping into neuroscience, performance theory and sociology, Bogart also recounts vivid stories from her own life. But as neuroscience indicates, the event of remembering what happened is in fact the creation of something new.

What's the Story

Essays about art, theater and storytelling

Anne Bogart

Routledge
Taylor & Francis Group

LONDON AND NEW YORK

First published 2014
by Routledge
2 Park Square, Milton Park, Abingdon, Oxon OX14 4RN

and by Routledge
711 Third Avenue, New York, NY 10017

Routledge is an imprint of the Taylor & Francis Group, an informa business

© 2014 Anne Bogart

British Library Cataloguing in Publication Data
A catalogue record for this book is available from the British Library

Library of Congress Cataloguing in Publication Data
Bogart, Anne, 1951–
What's the story : essays about art, theater and storytelling / by Anne Bogart.
p. cm.
1. Theater–Production and direction. 2. Creation (Literary, artistic, etc.) 3. Storytelling. 4. Arts–Miscellanea. I. Title.
PN2053.B595 2014
792.01–dc23
2013040768

ISBN: 978-0-415-74998-5 (hbk)
ISBN: 978-0-415-75000-4 (pbk)
ISBN: 978-1-315-78083-2 (ebk)

Typeset in Sabon
by Taylor & Francis Books

For Rena Chelouche Fogel

Contents

Acknowledgements

A special thank you to Rena Chelouche Fogel, who walked with me through every step in the realization of this book. Her taste, patience, love, intelligence and ability to see both large and small issues were all crucial. Thank you also to Brian Kulick, Todd London, Ellen Lauren, Janet Wong, Ross Wasserman, Julie Rossi, Leon Ingulsrud, Alona Fogel, Amlin Gray and Matthew Glassman for their supportive notes and ideas. Thank you to Megan Hiatt at Routledge for her sharp focus and attention. And finally thank you to Talia Rodgers for her continued belief in and support of the project of these books.

Introduction

Those who do not have power over the story that dominates their lives, the power to retell it, to rethink it, deconstruct it, joke about it, and change it as times change, truly are powerless, because they cannot think new thoughts.

(Salman Rushdie, novelist)

What's the Story is the third book in a series of essays about art and theater. In *A Director Prepares* and *And Then You Act*, I shared insights from my own encounters with art and my experiences directing theater. Mostly I shared these insights by telling the stories about how I first encountered them. But each time one recalls an event one gets further away from the original experience. And to recount a story based upon personal memory is actually an act of creation. The more times that I activate a memory, the more distanced the memory becomes from the perceived facts of the initial experience. This is simply the way the brain and memory works.

It is not enough to tell stories. There must be someone there to listen. Initially, I wrote the essays in order to communicate with fellow artists and to begin what I hoped would become a conversation. Also, I figured that, once told, I could then leave those particular stories behind me and go on to experience new ones. I promised myself that after publication I would stop telling the stories from the books. This turned out to be a difficult promise to keep because stories are such an efficient way of sharing hard-earned experiences, feelings, insights and lessons. Plus, I enjoy telling stories immensely.

We are telling stories all of the time. Our body tells a story. Our posture, our smile, our liveliness or fatigue, our stomach, our blank stare, our fitness, all speak, all tell a story. How we walk into a room tells a story. Our actions relate multiple stories. We invest our own energy into stories. Deprived of energy, stories die.

It is natural to adopt other people's stories to help create our identities and to fill in gaps in our own experience or intelligence. This can be helpful up to a point but it is easy to get stuck in other people's narrative structures. Stories become easily cemented and rendered inflexible, developing into assumptions upon which a life is lived. Without vigilance, stories simply become documented history and form, and their origins are forgotten. Rather than mechanically allowing other people's stories to guide our lives, it is possible to get involved and narrate from a state of passionate participation.

> Theater is a form of knowledge; it should and can also be a means of transforming society. Theater can help us build our future, rather than just waiting for it.
>
> (Augusto Boal, theater director, writer and politician)

During the course of the past several years we have experienced a seismic shift in the way the world functions. Any notion of a certain or stable or inevitable future has vanished. We are living in what the Polish philosopher Zygmunt Bauman calls "liquid modernity." No one's life is predictable or secure. We are confronted with challenges never previously encountered, and these challenges weigh heavily on the role and responsibilities of the individual in society. It is the onus of each one of us to adjust, shift and adjust again to the constant liquid environment of fluid and unending change. In the midst of all this reeling and realignment, the moment is ripe to activate new models and proposals for how arts organizations can flourish in the present climate and into an uncertain future. Can we begin to think of ourselves, rather than stagers of plays, as orchestrators of social interactions in which a performance is a part, but only a fragment of that interaction? Can we develop communities of individuals who are participants of an ongoing dialogue?

The most vital aspect of being alive and responsible in this new climate of "liquid modernity" is to recognize the power and significance of individual action. All of our thoughts and actions become, in due course, public. When we engage in a conversation with someone, even a telephone call, the impact does not end there. The conversation travels. We have no idea where it might stop or what our private action will engender on the shared public plane. Cultural change arises without our direct control. We *can* control our own individual contributions to the emergent migration or flow. We *can* affect the world around us in our every move and thought and action. If each one of us brings a dish to the table, a feast may ensue. In the case of the theater, a feast that is informed by the memories of what great theater might engender is an infinitely richer meal.

Be careful how you interpret the world; it's like that.

(Erich Heller, essayist)

We dream. And then occasionally we attempt to share our dreams with others. In recounting our dreams we impose narratives upon the barrage of images and notions that our dreams produce. We also make stories out of the blips and bleeps of our daytime existence. The human brain is a narrative-creating machine that takes whatever happens and imposes chronology, meaning, cause and effect. We manufacture reasons and explanations for everything that happens.

More important than the facts of any life is the meaning and significance that we attribute to those facts. How we frame and construct the narratives has a profound effect not only upon our own lives but also upon the lives of those around us. Jean-Paul Sartre wrote that there are two ways to go to the gas chamber: free or not free. We choose. We can choose to relate to our circumstances with bitterness or with openness. The stories that we tell determine nothing less than personal destiny. Both individually and collectively, we write the histories with the meaning that we attribute to the events around us. In the theater we are the inheritors of myriad stories from numerous cultures and scores of centuries. We are marked by the stories that we receive. They impress upon us their lessons that in turn change the neural structures of our brains.

On automatic pilot we tend to construct narratives that are imitations of other people's stories or copies of inherited assumptions from family, school, political and religious indoctrination or advertising. But, in fact, stories are one of the few aspects of our lives that, with a certain attentive will, we can control. It is possible to compose our own stories. We can choose how to outline and narrate the events that happen to us and the narratives that we devise can help prevent us from becoming powerless. But the option to take responsibility for our own stories requires effort, vigilance and accountability.

Chapter 1

Narrative

> All sorrows can be borne if you put them into a story or tell a story about them.
>
> (Karen Blixen, novelist)

When I was 16 years old I began to keep a journal. In addition to descriptions of my daily activities, I wrote poetry and song lyrics and generally tried to keep track of my wandering heart and romantic yearnings. Little by little the writing became a habit. During my year as a college sophomore in Athens, Greece, a friend who everyone called "the Flea," proposed a new technique for journal writing. "Write three observations every day," she said. I found the task challenging. It is easy to write, "Today I went to the bank and then to a taverna with the Flea." But to form an opinion and develop a point of view requires effort and imagination. "As I entered the bank I found the juxtaposition of my life to those on the streets outside uncomfortable. The homeless are more prevalent this year than last." Or, "The mood at the table in the basement taverna, our favorite one in the Kolonaki district, was more somber than usual. Perhaps the pressure of exams has distracted us all."

In writing the previous paragraph I turned the materials of my own life so many years ago into a story. I wrote and rewrote until the description felt like a journey, or story, for the reader. In telling a story I funnel my observations and feelings through a particular lens. The result is the distillation of experience into a communicative form, into expression. Without the process of compression and distillation, there is no expression, only description. And expression communicates more effectively than description.

I am a product of postmodernism, of deconstructionism, of a general rejection of hierarchical narrative and objective truth. For much of my life in the theater I have resisted the comfort and tyranny of stories. But the times are shifting. I would like to propose that we have reached the end of postmodernism. We are on the cusp of a new paradigm, as yet unnamed, only partially inhabited, unfamiliar and novel. The pecking order of top-down organizational structures and hierarchical control are losing strength. It is becoming increasingly clear that the hegemony of isolationism is not a solution to our present global circumstances. Our understanding of action and responsibility is changing. We know now that our tiniest gestures have large-scale effects, as do the outward ripples of a pebble thrown into a pond. In moments such as these, of upheaval and change, stories become necessary to frame our experiences. It is the role of the artist to "wright" new fictions. Those who can formulate the stories that make the world understandable will redefine the experience of those who live in it.

> Human beings like stories. Our brains have a natural affinity not only for enjoying narratives and learning from them but also for creating them. In the same way that your mind sees an abstract pattern and resolves it into a face, your imagination sees a pattern of events and resolves it into a story.
>
> (James Wallis, video-game designer)

Researchers have found that the human brain has a natural affinity for narrative construction. People tend to remember facts more accurately if they encounter them in the context of a story rather than in a list; and they even rate legal arguments as more convincing when built into a narrative rather than presented in a legal presentation.

From their ancient origins and continuing through today, stories bind societies by reinforcing common values and strengthening the ties of shared culture. But they do more than that. Stories give order and meaning to existence and are less costly than direct experience because with stories it is possible to collect information without having to personally undergo the experience. Also, fiction provides a playground and a workout for cognitive functionality. In the Darwinian sense, those who tell stories are sexually attractive to others, and stories, like taking drugs, give the teller a chemical charge.

The most significant human exchanges occur through narrative. Even a well-told bedtime story can permanently alter the synaptic pathways of the brain in the listener. I believe that the stories that we tell, about ourselves and about others, matter. The clarity with which I tell a story can affect what will eventually come to pass because I will end up living the narrative that I describe. What is the story I am telling? Does the story that I tell and retell inevitably become my particular experience and the experience of people around me?

It is possible that novelist Jeanette Winterson became a writer because she did not agree with the story that her mother told about her family and she did not concur with her mother's definition of what makes a good human being. Winterson needed to tell her own story in her own way, and writing became a battle about whose story would rule. She rewrote her story in a veiled fiction entitled *Oranges Are Not the Only Fruit*, a novel that became a bestseller in Britain, and more recently in an autobiography, *Why Be Happy When You Could Be Normal?* Perhaps the battle between Jeanette Winterson and her mother was a battle of interpretation. The parent struggled to maintain her own identity and the identity of her daughter, a person she invested in and described in her own way. The child attempted to rewrite the story into a tale that makes sense to her. And so, it seems to me, storytelling can be an act of survival.

The practice of storytelling begins in the day-to-day minutiae of one's own life. Because we are meaning-making machines, we translate our experiences into potent narratives. We tell stories to make sense of our experiences. Through this act of translation, we develop opinions and assumptions about how things are. The human impulse to tell one's own story is one of the basic human rights and freedoms in democratic societies. Speaking effectively, and communicatively, whether onstage, in poetry, in a book or in conversation, can free one from the prison of the past. Speaking a story can be an act of letting in light.

Think of the hero/prisoner in Plato's "Allegory of the Cave." A group of people lives chained inside a cave, facing a blank wall. They watch shadows projected on the wall thrown by things passing in front of a fire behind them, and they ascribe meaning to these shadow forms. A prisoner, freed from his shackles, walks out of the darkness of the cave into the blazing sunlight. What makes him a hero, and in Plato's case the best sort of politician, is that after witnessing the startling vision of trees and sun and landscape, he turns around and *re-enters* the cave to tell the story of his journey to others who had until then imagined that life is simply the shadows teasing them. He suffers their incomprehension but the act of return and his attempt to enthrall the others with the story of what he has seen and experienced in order to fire their imaginations is ultimately what makes him a hero.

The hunger for stories is not a body hunger, but it is a huge and fierce hunger, and it is as necessary for human well-being as food is for the body. We have to make stories and then we have to consume stories or our brains don't work right, and when we consume stories, we are consuming life. Stories carry energy, they make patterns in the way we think and behave, and we have to have them to live in a social order.

(Jo Carson, poet and playwright)

In the theater we construct journeys for audiences utilizing the tools of time and space. We create societies, tell stories and propose means by which people can live together with increased humanity, empathy and humor. An effective production communicates in ways that infiltrate the audience in multiple layers, weaving details and scenes, narration, imagery, symbolic action, plot and character. Learning to "wright" stories effectively is a lifetime study.

In the heat of a performance, the actors and the audience are readers and writers at the same moment. An actor reads the room, takes the temperature of the audience's listening and makes instantaneous decisions about how to, in turn, write upon the stage. The audience reads the actor's writing from one moment to the next. They collaborate in the joint effort of the creation of the theatrical event.

The human mind is tuned to detect patterns. A baby swiftly learns to read patterns in its surroundings and begins to write back. In "writing back," the mind attempts to craft ordered narratives from random input. The brain circuitry pores over incoming information, filters for patterns and arranges those patterns into stories. This inborn appetite for meaningful patterns in turn translates into a hunger for narrative.

In order to write effectively we must learn to read well because it is impossible to write anything without reading first. Great writers are effectively great readers. To read teaches one to write. Reading is a lifelong study. The substance of the world, its "literature," is vast and unendingly rich, a sea of multitudinous differences. To mature is to open up one's relation to the world through an increased ability to read creatively. The ongoing challenge for every artist is to remain fresh to the world, to continue to find novelty in each experience, even as the years pass by and one's perception tends to surrender to the assumptions about what and how "things" are.

Reading and writing is a joint effort that has consequences. When the writing is effective, that is to say when the art is effective, the reader's world, that is to say the receiver's world, expands to meet the writer's, and in that very interaction, the world is altered just a bit.

The essential tools for reading are a combination of focus and awareness. The two are not identical. Focus is a consciously directed attention. Awareness is a wider, spongier cognizance. When too focused we miss out on the flow of random, undigested bits that help us to understand the bigger picture. Without awareness, we miss a significant percentage of the creative process.

Jonathan Franzen, in his book of essays entitled *Farther Away*, describes his realization that in order to write the kind of book that he dreamed of writing but felt incapable of doing, he would have to become a different kind of writer and in order to do that he would have to become a different kind of person.

If we engage deeply enough in the experience, reading the writing of others can alter us profoundly. I believe that we can become "a different kind of person" simply by exposure to powerful writing, even within the duration of a novel or a play. Reading offers opportunities for transformation through our imaginative engagement with art. A lifetime of transformative reading can help one to become an effective agent of the artistic experience, to communicate with clarity and power and to become the writer one wants to become.

> A well-lived life should be worth attention. At the very least, you should find your own story engaging. In presenting yourself to yourself and others, then, you should keep in mind the rules that good playwrights follow. Like a good character – you should be making choices that are explicable – choices that appear to be coming from a mind in working order. Your choices should be reasonably coherent with each other, also, so as to support the thought that there is a real person – you – behind those choices.
>
> (Paul Woodruff, philosopher)

Whether or not there are any actual connections between the incidents we live through daily, our minds are designed to string these events into storylines. We produce reasons for our actions that seem rational and plausible, and yet the motives that we assign to our own actions are often fictions designed to help our lives make sense. But the stories that we tell others and ourselves about our lives end up becoming the lives we live. And so, I believe that the way we describe our lives and ourselves is a creative force behind the experience of life itself.

A friend wrote and prepared to direct his own film. A producer was in place, money had been raised, casting was complete and the crew had arrived on location. Just before the shooting began, the producer announced sheepishly that all of the funding had fallen through. Devastated, my friend and his wife went for a walk in a local graveyard. "What is the story we want to tell our children about this experience?" they asked themselves. Ultimately they decided to cash in their life savings and fund the project themselves. They chose the story that they wanted to tell, consciously put their resources in service of that story and realized a remarkable film entitled *Big Bad Love*.

Most of my days are lived within the confines of the evolving narratives that I spin about who I am. Therefore, "What is the story I want to tell?" is a pivotal question. The narratives that I choose determine the sort of life that I will live because I create who I am with the stories I tell. I write myself into existence by the stories that I tell about my life. I also write with my posture and with my manner of walking and speaking, and I write with words and with my actions. I write fuzzily or, with extra effort and deliberate thinking, I can write clearly. I impress myself upon and into others. I write and I am also written upon. My DNA writes upon me and my family writes upon me. I am written upon by the experiences that I undergo, by the people that I meet, the books that I read and the music that I listen to.

I am also an inheritor of great stories, myths and parables that formed who I am and how I think about the world, including my morality and ethics. Many of the stories that I tell are adaptations of these formidable fictions. But I can also be a transmitter of new stories. Perhaps I can think of my life as a play that I "wright." I construct and reconstruct narratives. Ultimately the story that I "wright" is a fragment of an interconnected accumulation of many stories by many other "wrighters" in a worldwide web of linked stories.

> When you change the way an individual thinks of himself, you change the way he lives in his community and thereby you change the community in some way.
>
> (Jo Carson, poet and playwright)

At the Theater Communications Group Conference in Baltimore in 2009, "Generation Y" representative Nadira Hira bounded onto the stage and announced that she would not be using any PowerPoint in her talk. "Hooray," I thought, "What a relief!" After several days of presentations and lectures with nonstop visual information displayed behind the speakers, I was relieved to be spoken to without technical support and accoutrements. Hira went on to explain that her generation is moving away from PowerPoint lectures because they understand the physical intensity of speaking directly to an audience.

What do they understand?

A PowerPoint presentation, with its bullet points, charts and graphs, activates a very small portion of the brain – the Broca and Wernicke areas. These brain regions process language. Words are decoded into meaning. That's it. When a PowerPoint presentation is in process, the brain shuts down to a small area of function.

In comparison, metaphor, storytelling and emotional exchange between people or portrayed between characters can stimulate the brain as a whole. Stories are journeys of the mind that provide the opportunity to enter into other people's thoughts and feelings. If I can engage a person's imagination, I will have managed to link our brains one to the other. Our brains synchronize, one with the other.

Our present-day culture is inundated with instantly available information and I am as addicted to the high of information as the next person. But what is the difference between apprehension and comprehension, between information received and information processed? Without the real experience of processing information, can insight, point-of-view or even transformations occur? I do not think so.

Telling stories is our way of coping, a way of creating shape out of a mess. It binds everyone together.

(Sarah Polley, filmaker)

I use stories as a method of teaching. By telling my own stories, the ones that have helped to shape my thinking and action, I can offer my students a slice of my original experience and insights. If interested enough and open to what I have to say, they can live vicariously through my own life-encounters. Of course they translate my experience with their own memories, associations, thoughts and desires. But in telling the stories, there is the chance that my brain might synchronize successfully with theirs. When our brains are properly synchronized, I am able to share my hard-won experiences with my students.

Princeton psychologist Uri Hasson calls this synchronization "brain-coupling." The listener's brain activity mirrors the speaker's. According to Hasson, the greater the coupling, the greater the mutual understanding. Communication between brains is made possible by a shared neural system that links the production of speech to the perception of speech. If receptive and if we use our imaginations, the stories that we hear can give us an approximate sensation of undergoing the experience itself.

Words are powerful stimulants of brain activity. By simply telling a story, I can plant ideas, thoughts and emotions into the listener's brain. If I tell the story effectively, I will have succeeded in stimulating a multitude of thoughts, sensations, feelings and associations in the receiver. Words describing motion stimulate the motor cortex, which is the area activated in the midst of actual motion. Likewise, the sensory cortex is aroused by descriptions or metaphors about touch and taste. In the thrall of a story not only are the language-processing parts of the brain activated, but also the identical synaptic activity that would happen if we were *actually* experiencing the events of the story.

> Stories, like conjuring tricks, are invented because history is inadequate to our dreams.
>
> (Steven Millhauser, novelist)

Stories are fragments of cause and effect linked together. The reason that stories work so well with humans is because stories are essentially a reflection of how we think. The brain constantly constructs narratives to explain day-to day experiences, supplying explanations of cause and effect by utilizing what has already been experienced and then linking all of those bits into new narratives. When we hear a new story, we apply it to the storehouse of our accumulated experiences or to our own personal stories or narratives.

Metaphor has the exceptional capacity to activate wide-ranging mental activity by stimulating the understanding of one element through the experience of another. In the imaginative hunt for similar experiences, metaphors can activate a part of the brain called the insula, which helps to identify analogous incidents of revulsion, pain, joy or whatever else held power over our attention previously. The French theater director Ariane Mnouchkine believes that theater is *all* metaphor.

During Suzuki and Viewpoints classes, SITI Company asks that the participants not take notes, even when watching. The act of recording takes one away from the direct experience of the very next thing that happens. We encourage participants to write notes after class but not during class. In class we ask for the full engagement of direct experience without the bookkeeping brain dominating. In order to benefit from direct experience, it's best not to limit the brain to the administration of facts.

In Paris, in 1971, writer Deirdre Bair met with the Irish playwright Samuel Beckett to request permission to conduct extensive interviews with him for what would become a definitive biography. Beckett granted Bair consent but on the condition that she not tapercord or even take notes. Bair agreed nervously. During nearly three hundred interviews, she listened closely to Beckett, who described countless details about his life and work. Then Bair rushed back to her hotel room to quickly tapercord her memories of Beckett's words that day. From these experiences she constructed a readable and consequential biography, published in 1978.

Perhaps Beckett understood that an unmediated connection between Bair and him would reap more riches than standard interview techniques that depend upon recording and recounting. Perhaps he valued their human connection more than any chronicle of reported facts. Perhaps what happened between them, together with Bair's reconstructed memories of their direct encounters, is what makes her biography of Beckett successful and interesting.

A talent for speaking differently, rather than for arguing well, is the chief instrument of cultural change.

(Richard Rorty, philosopher)

Artists and scientists are activists. They look at the world as changeable and they look upon themselves as instruments for change. They understand that the slice of world they occupy is only a fragment but that the fragment is intrinsically connected to the whole. They know that action matters.

I am interested in using narratives consciously to make things happen. After 20 years with me as the sole artistic director, SITI Company voted to change its leadership structure. We realized that in order to thrive in the future we must reassess how we make decisions and how we communicate with one another. We determined to create a shared leadership model. I presently share the artistic leadership of the company with Ellen Lauren and Leon Ingulsrud.

The initial steps towards shared leadership were awkward. How do we explain this new model to the world? How do we organize the day-to-day implementation of the plan? How do we describe ourselves? What are our titles? We fumbled a bit. Together with Executive Director Megan Wanlass and her administrative ensemble, we tried to act as much as we could as a shared leadership team, but without clear accountabilities and guidelines, we felt like we were simply improvising while awaiting a new structure. One day Ellen walked into the SITI office, looked around and began to rearrange the furniture. Literally. She forged space for two new workstations – one for her and one for Leon. And then both of them got down to work. Suddenly the nuts and bolts of shared leadership became clearer and more fluid. Architecture helps. So does action. The more we act in concord with the narrative that we are trying to tell, the more the story, what is initially a fiction, becomes a reality. Speak the narrative that you want to realize and then find the appropriate actions to make that story a reality.

Starting somewhere in the middle of the twentieth century, the American theater began to develop an inferiority complex. The stories chosen to describe the field weakened and these narratives began to make theater professionals seem like beggars, like lesser citizens. The American theater, thus conditioned by habit and faulty narratives not to expect much municipal support or public endorsement, has weakened. If it is true that expectations create experience, our low expectations have created a self-fulfilling prophecy. But I believe that with serious, conscious, deliberate thinking and action, it is possible to alter expectations and change the narratives.

In order to consciously and slowly "re-wright" the story that we are telling about the American theater, initially it is helpful to slow down. In his book *Thinking Fast and Slow*, Daniel Kahneman distinguishes between fast, impulsive thinking and slow, deliberate thinking. Slow thinking requires far more effort and attention. Slow thinking alters the body's blood flow, increases muscular tension and even dilates the eyes. Slow thinking also tends to make things happen.

During the height of the recent recession, an article in the Science section of the *New York Times* counseled the newly unemployed to spend their days as if they were going to work, even if they had nowhere to go. The article encouraged the unemployed to dress up, leave the house and spend time actively, even if this meant sitting in a local Starbucks searching for work online. In order to move into the next phase of their lives, the key is not to *act* unemployed.

Leon Ingulsrud, one of the co-artistic directors of SITI Company, told me about how he got hired to direct a play in Ireland. The actress Olwen Fouéré said that she chose him for the job because during the interview he was already acting like the director of the production.

> If we could change ourselves, the tendencies in the world would also change. As a man changes his own nature, so does the attitude of the world change towards him. ... We need not wait to see what others do.
>
> (Mahatma Gandhi, leader)

To initiate change I must be a model for that change. First I have to cultivate a conscious awareness of my own habitual patterns, and then I have to commit an act of conscious re-framing. I must act like the person that I want to be. How I conceive of myself determines how others conceive of me. I construct the story that I want to tell.

Is it possible to feel successful by acting successful? While it is true that our size, skin color and the timbre of our voices are already prescribed, it is also true that we can choose our posture and the tempo of our entrance as well as the way we wear our clothes. We make an impression upon others as we enter a room. We make an impression by how we occupy space, what we pay attention to and to whom we connect.

A self is probably the most impressive work of art we ever produce, surely the most intricate. For we create not just one self-making story but many of them, rather like T.S. Eliot's rhyme "We prepare a face to meet/The faces that we meet." The job is to get them all into one identity, and to get them lined up over time.

(Jerome Bruner, psychologist)

Two people in the identical situation can interpret their experience in completely different ways. In line in a grocery store, trapped in an elevator, on a crowded plane, caught with no umbrella in a rainstorm or in a hospital waiting room, I cannot always control what happens to me but I can influence the story about what is happening. I cannot determine what illnesses or challenges might happen, but I can develop an attitude in relation to these issues. With consciousness and restraint, I can choose how to think about my circumstances and I can temper my actions in a way that contributes to rather than diminishes the welfare of my fellow travelers.

David Logan in his book *Tribal Leadership* suggests that groups and the individuals within these groups tend to function in one of five possible paradigmatic stages.

Stage one: *"Life sucks."* This attitude, according to Logan, can result from the group experience of, say, prison. Prison is a difficult paradigm to transcend and groups in prison are understandably susceptible to "life sucks," which can result from the inmates' daily experience of violent action or seething inaction.

Stage two: *"My life sucks."* In line at the DMV everything feels gray and impossible. No one is there to help anyone and one is not about to contribute either.

Stage three: *"I'm great and you're not."* Life is a Darwinian struggle revolving around "who's on top," embedded with competition and one-upmanship. The world is a place of competition and struggle for survival.

Stage four: *"We're great."* Logan offers the example of the Zappos company, where employees celebrate one another in the context of the corporate culture. The sensibility is a group culture working for a united cause.

Finally, the highest paradigm,

Stage five: "*Life is great.*" The impulse in South Africa to organize the Truth and Reconciliation Commission is a perfect example. Only in this humanitarian frame of mind can a group tend to such compassionate and ingenious measures.

I believe that how I describe my life matters not only to my own experience but also to the experiences of others. What is the story that I am telling? Do I choose to say, "*My life sucks?*" Do I choose to say, "*Life is great?*" Or do I swing jaggedly from one to another? The choice – if I am lucky, rigorous, and attentive enough – is mine. But in order to "wright" a good narrative, I first need to create the kind of ego that can create one.

Chapter 2

Heat

The flow of water carves rock, a little bit at a time. And our personhood is carved, too, by the flow of our habits.

(Jonathan Safran Foer, novelist)

The Brazilian theater director Augusto Boal, inspired by the ideas of Lope de Vega, said, "Theatre is the passionate combat of two human beings on a platform." Passion, according to Boal, is a feeling for someone or something, or an idea that we prize more highly than our own life.

The theater, normally chock-full of heat and passion, generally concerns itself with conflict, confrontation and defiance. A drama typically unfolds in a symphonic interplay of opposing forces and actions in which characters have an investment in situations for which they venture their lives and their beliefs as well as their moral and political choices. Derived from the Latin verb *pati*, which means to suffer, passion implies intense feeling, enthusiasm, compelling emotion or desire.

Neuroscientist Antonio Damasio proposed that while emotions and feelings can cause havoc in the processes of reasoning, their absence is no less damaging. The passions, he concludes, "have a say on how the rest of the brain and cognition go about their business." Emotion and heat seal the experience and create lasting memories. With passion, these memories, created in the brain in the heat of experience, become stable and in turn generate personal morals and ethics.

Passion is engendered not by feeling or emotion, but rather by action. Taking a risk or hazarding one's life for moral or political choices creates the kind of heat that generates strong passions. The act of engagement creates heat. Physical practice creates heat. Meeting challenging obstacles creates heat. Practicing commitment and investment generates heat. Action arising from authentic curiosity produces heat.

But passion and heat can also be generated through the act of restraint. When animal instincts run high, when adrenalin and the fight-or-flight instinct are elevated, it is possible to exercise self-control, to use the imagination to restrain and contain the intense emotions within form or etiquette. Chivalry and the chivalric code, for example, advocated conscious restraint in the face of danger.

A gym for the soul

At a SITI Company holiday party, I was sitting on the floor next to Jason Hackett, a great friend of the company who had recently joined the SITI board, bringing his expertise in marketing and branding to help our trajectory. Both of us were hunched over plates of holiday food when Jason said, "Tell me why my friends should come to see a SITI Company production." I took a deep breath and began to talk about how our plays engage audiences with issues of contemporary interest and how they are like theatrical essays on relevant subjects. Jason interrupted me. "No," he said, "my friends would not be interested in any of that. Exactly what will attract them to attend a SITI production?" I took another deep breath and tried again. I spoke about the extraordinary collaborative spirit of SITI Company and how our ensemble approach proposes ways that social systems might function in harmony together. Again Jason shook his head. "No," he said, "none of this would sell a ticket." I was getting agitated and continued to propose reasons that might attract Jason's friends to a SITI Company production. Finally, I blurted out, "We offer a gym for the soul." At last Jason smiled and exclaimed, "Yes, that would interest them. Now I know how to talk about SITI."

In the hyper-mediated environment that we presently inhabit, energizing personal and communal experiences are becoming increasingly priceless. Consumer culture promises a frictionless existence. And yet we are generally not energized by experiences that ask little of us. Consumer culture encourages us to celebrate the easy-to-come-by, the pre-digested and the ready-made. But energy increases in direct proportion to the engagement demanded. Meeting personal challenges and overcoming obstacles generates power and heat. Engagement and involvement create energy. We are energized and widened by experiences that ask for our investment, whether in time, imagination or mental and emotional facilities.

Each obstacle or challenge encountered requires concomitant expansion. We have to literally make space for the heat of the encounter. At a classic gym, for example, the investment of energy and focus required to meet resistances guarantees an increase of muscular size and strength. Neurologists have found that London taxi drivers develop a larger posterior hippocampus than non-drivers because the demands of spatial acuity in these drivers develop the parts of the brain that engage in spatial issues. The art experience and the theater experience, gyms for the soul, generate heat and exercise the imagination, empathy, creative thinking, patience and tolerance. A gym for the soul is a place where personal investment is required and the return is real.

My first encounter with the work of Dutch director Ivo Von Hove was a production of *More Stately Mansions*, an early play of Eugene O'Neill, at the New York Theatre Workshop in 1997. The play is long, nearly four hours, and rarely performed. At the beginning of the evening the actors walked out onto the stage, bowed to the audience, bowed to one another and then all moved to the side of the stage to sit in folding metal chairs, except for the actress Joan MacIntosh, who faced the audience, took a deep breath and launched into the initial eight-page monologue at top speed. I jerked forward in my seat in surprise. I was seized and challenged and I did not want to miss a word. After a few minutes I began to hear the familiar slap-slap of seats being abandoned as members of the audience left the theater in droves. Probably more than one quarter of the audience walked out in the first ten minutes of the play. Filled with excitement, I stayed because I sensed that the experience would ask a great deal of me and I hoped that my investment of attention would be worthwhile. Indeed, those of us who stayed enjoyed a theatrical journey that was dense, poetic and thrilling.

It took a Dutch director to teach me yet another lesson about what it means to be an American artist. As a theater director in a populist culture, I am inclined to start easy and save the hard bits for later on when I think that the audience is prepared to deal with the challenges. But in fact an audience learns how to watch a play in the first few moments of a production. As theater-makers, we cast the audience. We signal how to listen; we say to them, "This is what is expected of you." And this is exactly what Ivo Von Hove did from the beginning of *More Stately Mansions*. His message to the audience was "if you want to benefit from this experience, you will have to engage. You are going to have to invest."

The financial world uses powerful words that are also useful to discuss the merits of the theater experience: *trust, investment, return, interest, dividend, benefits* and so on. I go to the theater because I *trust* the company, the artists involved or the critics. Once there, the actors ask me to *invest* my attention, my mind and my imagination in what they are doing. If I do not invest, I will not enjoy a *return*. Appreciation is accrued, multiplied by investment, trust and patience. The investment has the potential to create *interest*. Interest generates even more interest. Appreciation is accrued. I receive a *return*. I receive a *dividend*. I become a *beneficiary*.

Room is a one-woman show based largely upon the non-fiction writings of Virginia Woolf. We have performed the production for many years in many theaters. The material is challenging – a veritable gym for the soul. I watch the audience enter the theater to find their seats. Amidst them in the auditorium, brightly lit, sits Ellen Lauren, her back erect and her focus towards the stage. As the play begins, Ellen stands abruptly and says to the assembled, "Good evening." Then she steps up onto the stage and begins what at first sounds like a lecture and then transforms gradually into a poetic symphony and an affecting cry of the soul. I always feel empathy for the audience during the first 20 minutes of the show. The production asks for investment from each individual audience member. Without that investment, the audience receives little in return. With the investment, Ellen's depth dive can guarantee a rich reward. The soul and the mind of each audience member willing to make an investment in the evening expands and multiplies in the heat of the demand for engagement.

Getting what you "want"

> I admit, I'm driven but I'm driven by desire and that's the formula. Desire is so powerful, like you are propelled as if from a canon. Desire to me is the driving force, but action is the result.
>
> (Phyllis Sues, 90-year-old dancer)

We want something. We desire something. We are frustrated by the lack of "it." We marinate in our frustration. The frustration drives us towards a vision of what it is that we desire or long for. The more frustrated we are, the more motivated we are to achieve what is lacking.

My own intense youthful desires were activated by the combination of a compelling dissatisfaction with my life situation and an early exposure to books. I was brought up in a naval family and every year or two we picked up and moved to a new city or a different country. Books became a great solace and rescue from the sense of isolation that resulted from losing beloved friends every time we moved. Literature and particularly biographies were an escape from what felt like the unbearable realities of family and school. The books also proposed parallel universes promising flight, adventure, rescue and nothing less than alternate existences. These books activated a compelling desire in me for all of those things. I felt a lack, an immense craving and a gnawing frustration, which in turn created an intense desire and appetite for alternatives to a life that seemed preordained.

Many successful comedians describe watching the *Tonight Show* starring Johnny Carson as children, in front of the family TV, longing to be there, on Johnny's couch, part of that exciting world. I am convinced that their longings and their desire to be "there" are part of what gave them the necessary fuel to advance in their cutthroat careers.

The heat of longing and frustration are necessary ingredients to the achievement of a vision. We cook it and it cooks us. Frustration and longing linked to desire furnish the fuel, the energy to proceed. If we do not undergo enough frustration, perhaps we will not cultivate the determination and endurance that gives our action-in-the-world substance.

And yet, perhaps paradoxically, the Buddhists propose that pain is caused by personal attachment to desire. And so, although I recognize the value of pain and frustration, I consciously and vigilantly police my own burning desires in order to live closer to and in harmony with the realities of the unfolding present moment. I try to stay free from what I perceive as a prison of "wanting."

I have often suggested that the word "want" is killing the American theater. I feel that in rehearsal we tend to employ the word excessively. A director says to an actor, "now I *want* you to walk downstage," or an actor asks a director, "is this what you *want*?" We unconsciously set up parent–child relationships between the director and actors. I have proposed that this manner of speaking is an endemic and a serious spiritual and political problem in our field.

In a recent open forum in the SITI Company studio in midtown, I mentioned my problem with the word "want" in the American theater. Present in the room were Stacy Klein and Carlos Uriona of the Double Edge Theater in Western Massachusetts. Both jumped into the conversation vehemently. "But our desires and wants are what drive *all* of our work and achievements," they said, almost as one. The more I thought about their point, the more I recognized that indeed their considerable achievements with Double Edge Theater are probably largely attributable to the elixir and heat of their shared desire. From nothing, over the past 20 years, Double Edge transformed a dilapidated farm in the midst of cow country into a destination for theater people and theater lovers everywhere. They created a theater center with renovated barns as performance spaces and rehearsal halls. They developed an acting company and mentored countless students, apprentices and interns. They found funding and support in the vicissitudes of shifting economic climates. They have involved their surrounding farm community and generated a love of theater that did not exist beforehand by incorporating local artisans – their food, textiles, stoneworking and so on – into their productions.

I also realized that the most compelling and satisfying life achievements, experiences and relationships that I have enjoyed are directly related to deep-seated desires. Indeed my career in the theater owes a great deal to an intense longing for what always felt to be just beyond my reach. As a girl, the circus that I wanted to run away to, the exotic community that I wanted to be a part of or the rarified atmosphere that I wanted to breathe regularly felt tantalizingly close and yet distant, possible and yet impossible to locate. Perhaps this is why I moved to New York City after college.

Desire arises from an inspiring sense of lack. But perhaps this sense of lack in our day-to-day lives can be the inspiration for our actions. Perhaps it is the gap between what we want and the way that things actually are that is actually our link, our connection to the world. Perhaps what matters most is what we make out of the frustrations that we feel. Perhaps frustration, longing and desire are also part of the recipe required for an artist to engage in interpretation and re-interpretation, transforming the quotidian into the sublime.

> Feeling and longing are the motive forces behind all human endeavor and human creations.
>
> (Albert Einstein, theoretical physicist)

In Amsterdam I saw a striking still life painted by Rembrandt van Rijn suspended above a glass case that contained the same objects that he used as a model for the picture. The contrast between what felt like a drab collection of random objects in the case and the stunning luminescent painting that seemed imbued with nothing less than intense energy and life gave me pause and clarified something I had been curious about. I had been thinking about the power of art to transform the frustrations and irritations of daily life into a realm of grace and to embody, through arrangement, composition, light, color and shade, nothing less than the secret elixir of life itself.

We encounter daily frustrations, irritations and obstacles. Perhaps we feel hampered and limited by our hit-and-miss upbringing, our apparent limitations and our imperfect ongoing circumstances. And yet Rembrandt's still life painting demonstrates that it is within our power to transform the random, the everyday, the frustrating and the prosaic into an arrangement instilled with grace and poetry. Is it the arrangement of these objects that lends such a spiritual quality to the painting? Is it the sensation of light captured upon canvas? How did Rembrandt transform the quotidian into an uplifting vision of life?

It was during my own teenage years that I began to look beyond the catalogue of Disney movies and naval base culture that was my daily existence and started to imagine something different. Happily, music, visual art and theater followed my exposure to books and were equally galvanizing, helping to locate specific targets for my arrows of desire. At the age of 15, a pivotal event occurred that provided my "Johnny Carson" moment. A school outreach program took my high school class in a yellow school bus from Middletown to Providence, Rhode Island to see a play at the Trinity Repertory Company. During the play, Shakespeare's *Macbeth*, my entire being reached towards the stage and simply longed to be part of that community. Not to necessarily be *on* the stage, but to be conjoined with the rarified world that was teeming up there. This new object of desire felt close and yet so distant simultaneously. And suddenly I had a target, I had a vision, I had something specific to work towards.

The process of assuaging the intense desires and realizing my dreams required time and perseverance. I waited. I worked and I learned, step by step. I soaked in what felt like a constantly accelerating well of frustration and longing. But the longing gave me perseverance and passion. I studied and practiced and made slow progress towards my desire – to direct theater.

Immediate gratification is the tantalizing prize of living in our current on/off/ping/ring-tone culture. The distance between what we desire and the fulfillment of that desire is rapidly shrinking. We acquire objects, information, music, books and clothes, whatever sparks a whiff of desire, with a single click. Our digital technologies empower us to make so many choices about so many things and so quickly. But the instantaneous nature of digital choice also thwarts our efforts to stay fully connected to our greater through-lines and to one another.

Waiting is not encouraged by the culture that we presently inhabit. We click once to satisfy the longings and desires that are, for the most part, manufactured by ubiquitous advertising campaigns, multi-national corporations and product placement. Perhaps a significant step has gone missing. Perhaps we are lacking the dissatisfaction that craves time. Perhaps it is the heat of frustration and the sensation of lack that intensifies personal desire, which in turn supports our development as artists. Perhaps if we do not feel enough lack and frustration, we will not fight long enough to realize our hard-won vision.

Getting started

How to begin? How do I presume to begin? Where do I start and why do I even try, in light of what Virginia Woof calls "the world's notorious indifference"? Each artist has a different approach to beginning.

One week before the launch of rehearsals for a recent new production, I set aside a Sunday at home to complete the final steps of preparation. I had planned for no disturbances; I scheduled no meetings and expected a full day of concentrated work on the project. But when the Sunday arrived, I simply pissed the day away. I did everything imaginable except for the crucial preparation I had planned to accomplish. I watched You-Tube videos, I read magazine articles, I wrote emails, I procrastinated by talking to Rena many times on the telephone in London and I took a nap. The next morning, I awoke furious with myself. Am I lazy? Undisciplined? How could I let this happen? How could I waste a very specially assigned day? After a helpful telephone conversation about the issue with my beloved Rena, who proposed that I think in depth about my choice to let the day pass without working, I realized that my inaction was simply due to terror. I am terrified to begin a new project. I am frightened of the blank page.

I believe that I am not alone in my terror. I find great comfort in Picasso's proposition that the first stroke on the canvas is *always* a mistake and that the remainder of the work on the canvas is the attempt to fix that mistake. Peter Brook wrote that the entire reason for the first day of rehearsal is simply to get to the second day of rehearsal. I understand this sentiment, although for me the initial day of rehearsal is key because it contains a compressed version of the entire journey of the upcoming rehearsal process. From my perspective, it is within that first day of rehearsal that the DNA of an entire production process is born. No pressure, right?

Several years ago, sound designer Darron West traveled from New York City to London to work with the Improbable Theatre Company on a new project that became *The Hanging Man*. Darron made his way with his backpack and heavy sound gear directly to the Improbable's studio from the airport and walked in to find the directors and the entire company lying on their backs on the studio floor with eyes closed. The walls were covered with scrawled upon Post-it notes and drawings. Phelim McDermott, one of the co-directors, picked up his head and opened his eyes just enough to see that Darron was in the room, patted the floor and said, "Join us." Darron put down his gear and joined the company on the floor and closed his eyes. "So Darron, based on what little you know right now and letting your imagination run wild, how does *The*

Hanging Man begin?" Darron proposed a few ideas and others joined in, thinking laterally. After a couple of hours, Phelim propped up onto his elbows and said, "OK, right, well then, how about a spot of tea and some lunch?" So they all stood up and trotted off to a local pub. After lunch they returned to the studio to lie back down again on their backs and continue to brainstorm the new project into existence. At the end of the day new Post-its with show ideas were added to the already crowded walls of the rehearsal room.

In many ways I envy Darron's experience in London, the days of lying on one's back, dreaming a project into being. But my process with SITI Company is quite different than the ways of the Improbable Theatre Company. I arrive at the first rehearsal jittery, nervous and buzzing with ideas, notions, associations, metaphors, images and whatever the months of preparation, research and study have ignited in me. I am bursting to share them. I usually spend the first few hours sharing every thought in my head to the assembled, speaking the world of the play into shared consciousness. After that, we begin to brainstorm together, free associate and to question every notion. And after that, we start the process of generating stage moments that either "land" within the world of the play that we are imagining, or not.

Once I have communicated all of my research, thoughts, ideas and notions on the initial day of rehearsal, I am able to move on to the second day, certainly with a plan but also blank, available to where the process needs to move and without the expectation or assumption that any of my initial ideas will actually come into being. Full of hope, I listen and respond to what happens moment by moment. Collectively, we throw ideas, moments and shapes up against the wall, onto the stage, to see what sticks. Ultimately, I feel that all of the planning simply gives me the right to walk into the rehearsal studio on that first day. The rest is listening and responding.

For me, beginning is simultaneously exciting and harrowing. My blood churns rapidly; my body is full of energy and a certain tension. I feel awkward, ill-equipped and uncomfortable but also grateful for the engagement. The effort is real. Perhaps, as in life, new beginnings should be attempted with regularity, all the way through the rehearsal process. Can the final week of rehearsal still be approached with what the Buddhists call "beginner's mind"?

I have learned that in the midst of my panic when launching a new project, it is best to start with something small and doable and build upon that. If what Picasso proposed is true, that the first stroke on the canvas is *always* a mistake, it is best to get on with the mistake, without delay, earlier rather than later. Write one sentence, make one choice or point at something and say "Yes." And then, as the process unfolds, and as long as I keep at it and stay attentive and resolute, making adjustments to each mistake, things eventually fall into place.

Deep practice

> If you don't push, nothing happens. Life is much more interesting when you make an effort.
>
> (Ai Wei Wei, visual artist)

The practice of theater requires a combination of technique, content and passion. Like a three-legged milking stool, if one of the legs is missing, the entire enterprise will collapse. Without the ingredient of the artist's passion for the material, no amount of craft or technique will help to convey the content. Similarly, without having something to say and a point of view, neither passion nor technique is sufficient.

Most art forms require rigorous ongoing practice of technique. Musicians, visual artists and dancers train daily. But acting schools, especially in the United States, do not encourage daily practice after graduation. Without a challenging practice, we are all inclined to become victims of our own habits and assumptions. And habits and assumptions are the enemies of art.

Practice changes the actual makeup of the body because new and lasting neural pathways can be forged in the heat of the practice. If the practice is deep and intense, the neural pathways that are created have a chance to endure over time. Deep practice requires enough motivation and energy to sustain the many, many critical hours of engagement. What supports maintaining motivation in the heat of practice is an image of the possible results plus the intensity of emotion felt when encountering the initial inspiration. This image becomes a model: a particular quality of orchestral sound, the fictional intensity of a great novel or the acting talent and abilities that inspire and set the imagination on fire. The image is then joined to the emotion that transpired in the initial encounter. Then, through practice, sweat and repetition, falling down and getting up again, the construction of new neural pathways begins.

Rote practice is not deep practice. Deep practice is slow, demanding and uncomfortable. To practice deeply is to live deliberately in a space that is uncomfortable but with the encouraging sense that progress can happen. Deep practice is not rushed. Constant critical feedback is essential. Over time the effort alters neural pathways and increases skill.

Fuck you Anne

I conducted a workshop with acting students at the Mozarteum in Salzburg, Austria. During our initial days together, I complained to the actors that they were far too careful and polite. Trying hard to please me, a guest director from abroad, their work was simply too accommodating. "Sie brauchen mehr 'Fuck you Anne'," I said ("You need more 'Fuck you Anne'"). Initially the actors were shocked when I spoke these words. I had been conducting the workshop in German but when it came to the words "Fuck you Anne" I spoke in English. They understood the words but were surprised that I had uttered them. Little by little, the actors came to understand that I wanted them to stop trying to please me and, instead, own the stage and seize each moment with greater alacrity and force. Gradually they learned to appreciate the space and freedom that I offered them and they began to work with a delightful and outrageous passion and defiance.

The actors' initial reticence is not an Austrian or German predisposition, rather a general tendency in the theater everywhere. Actors, programed to be polite and accommodating, should develop more autonomy and spirit. As a parting gift, after our final public presentation, the Mozarteum actors gathered around and presented me with a silver-framed print with bold black letters on bright yellow paper: "Fuck You Anne." The sign is now displayed in the hallway next to my office at Columbia University because it was hard won and meaningful to me. I am proud of it.

When I give a note to an actor, I do not want the actor to simply do what I describe. My note is meant to add perspective, not to be prescriptive. As a director, my job is to propose big, wide and penetrating questions and to welcome any ensuing disagreement or even rebellion. My job is to transcend my own agenda in order to see the wider context and my job is to cultivate the kind of spaciousness where permission is possible. I try to create the room in which everyone is both participating and responsible.

The film director Michelangelo Antonioni declared that he never gave an actor an honest note because he did not want the actor to simply do what he was told to do. He invariably lied to actors when addressing their questions. Unlike Antonioni, I do not want to lie but I do want to give a note that moves the target a little further away.

I think of the actor as an astronaut out in space while the director is in the control tower. The actor swings weightless through the cosmos experiencing the shifting spectacle of the earth and the universe. "Try moving to the right," I say from the control tower down on earth. The actor moves right to experience yet more uncharted territory. The actor's job, and this is key, is not solipsistic. It is undertaken in order to report with great clarity, from the heat of his or her experience in space, to the audience on earth.

The relationship between training, rehearsal and performance

What is the point of all the discipline, hard work and training? What does the training and preparation have to do with rehearsing a play and with performance? The training and the discipline and the sweating and the study and the memorizing are not the end point, but rather the entry. The preparation is what gives one the permission to take up space and make wild, surprising and untamed choices. In the quest for artistic freedom and agency it is impossible to walk into a rehearsal room uninhibited, unburdened. We are generally chained down by habits and assumptions and by the fear of the new. Permission is what we earn by the sweat, training, preparatory work and dedication.

In 1967 Jerzy Grotowski, along with his lead actor Ryszard Cieslak, led a four-week workshop at New York University, an event that ultimately changed the face of the American theater. After the workshop, some of the young American actors and directors who had taken part in the workshop were so galvanized and inspired by the experience that they formed theater companies that eventually became highly influential on the American theater landscape, including Andre Gregory's Manhattan Project and Richard Schechner's Performance Group.

The American participants were smitten by the enigmatic Grotowski and even perhaps more so by the intense physicality of the training. Grotowski and Cieslak introduced *les plastiques et corporels*, training exercises that helped the actors to transcend habitual movement patterns and get in touch with their basic biological impulses. When Grotowski departed, the Americans proceeded to incorporate *les plastiques et corporels* directly into their first productions. Literally. What the American participants did not seem to understand from Grotowski were his following words, which were chronicled by one of the participants, Tom Crawley: "The physical exercises are but a jumping-off place for an actor's own creativity, for his own exploration of himself and his own experience."

In 1969, Grotowski and his company were invited back to the United States to perform two plays: *The Constant Prince* and *Akropolis*. The American actors and directors were astonished to see none of the training, no *plastiques et corporels*, actually visible in the productions.

The Polish company performed plays that presented characters and clear dramatic situations. The exercises were nowhere to be seen. The Americans realized that *les plastiques et corporels* were simply training, a practice, not meant for audience consumption.

I find a similar misunderstanding about the difference between training, rehearsal and performance in our contemporary theater scene. The Viewpoints, one of the two systems of training practiced and taught by SITI Company, are often confused as either a rehearsal technique and/or performance. To me, the Viewpoints are not a technique to stage plays any more than a ballet barre practice provides a way to compose a dance. Nevertheless, there seems to be a great deal of curiosity about how the Viewpoints are used to direct or devise new work.

The Viewpoints are indeed useful as training, providing actors the opportunity to practice together regularly. Originally developed by choreographer Mary Overlie in the late 1970s and very influential throughout the theater world today, the Viewpoints are an improvisational study and practice of the subtleties of spatial and temporal issues in performance. Using the ingredients of time and space, the Viewpoints allow actors to practice generating fiction collaboratively on the blank canvas of the rehearsal hall floor. The Viewpoints encourage deep listening and help to cultivate an actor's ability to render action outwardly visible and inwardly transparent, emphasizing technical precision while embracing spontaneity and unpredictability. And the Viewpoints promote ensemble creation. But at its heart the Viewpoints are improvisation and I do not believe that improvisation is, by nature, art. To me, theater is born after something is fixed, decided upon and then *repeated*. The theater is the art of repetition. The artist's task is to bring back to life, to resurrect, what has been annihilated by the decisive act of choice. And the act of decisiveness can be brutal. In the heat of decision, the gentle life-breath that gave birth to the impulse is killed. I believe that the necessary act of resurrection is when the real art is born. A successful production is one in which moments that have been carefully selected, set and artfully arranged nevertheless feel natural, full of life and, to an audience, spontaneous.

Although I resist the notion of the Viewpoints as a method to stage plays, I do find them useful in the process of rehearsal. In the initial half-hour of rehearsal, the SITI Company trains in both Suzuki and Viewpoints. An open Viewpoints improvisation provides the opportunity to activate and embody ideas under consideration without the onus of staging the play. Before the improvisation I share impressions and questions about the play without having a practical sense of where they might belong in the production. The Viewpoints allow for freely associative, embodied thinking about how elements that do not necessarily belong together rationally might be activated and juxtaposed within the grammar and syntax of time and space. The improvisations provide the opportunity to explore freely, ultimately enriching the compositional language of what we eventually fix or stage.

After training, we proceed to rehearse the production. We do not improvise. We rehearse scenes in the order of the play, except for songs and dances, which require daily rehearsal. We pay attention to psychology, motivation, spatial and temporal choices, gesture, physical action and dramaturgy. We often stop to discuss the intricacies of dialogue, context and psychology.

The process of rehearsal is the process of subtracting, of taking away whatever is in the way of seeing and hearing the play clearly. A key ingredient in any rehearsal process is, precisely, to not know the answers in advance. I feel that training, the heat of practice, is an ongoing necessity in the theater and exists in order to promote a constant reminder of the crucial question: How to rally the courage, strength and concentration to face a blank canvas with humility, vulnerability and openness?

Meeting in the heat of constructed situations

> "Looking deeply" means observing something or someone with so much concentration that the distinction between observer and observed disappears. The result is insight into the true nature of the object.
>
> (Thich Nhat Hanh, Zen Buddhist monk)

In our media-saturated culture, it is essential to be alert to the isolation and the desensitization of the spirit that we are prone to and, as artists, to propose alternatives. In a world of commerce and meritocracy we find ourselves disconnected from one another, obsessed with material gain and the accumulation of prestige. The performing arts offer an alternative. What does it mean to approach one another with awareness in the energized space of unmediated encounters?

Guy Debord, in his seminal book *The Society of the Spectacle* (1967), proposed an antidote to the deadening impact of capitalist spectacle in what he named "constructed situations," which calls on artists to create moments that coax people out of passivity, rendering them the co-creators of what promises to be, according to Debord, a less mediocre life. The "constructed situations" are temporary and highly dependent upon context. The present-day Occupy movement is a great proponent of constructed situations, calling for specific collective actions to happen at significant crossroads of global culture. Since its inception as Occupy Wall Street, the movement has spread worldwide. Generally the organizers announce a time and a place for "constructed situations," at, for example, a traffic intersection connecting to a commercial bridge, a bank or a factory. People gravitate to these places and participate within this context. There is no apparent prescribed narrative. What happens is meant to be spontaneous and mostly unscripted.

One of the most interesting current practitioners of Debord's notion of "constructed situations" is the young Anglo-German artist Tino Sehgal, who has created "acoustic" events at museums around the world in which usually large groups of "interpreters" carry out his instructions, which range from talking directly to museum visitors to singing, sitting, walking and running through the space together. Interested in fleeting gestures, the human voice, social interaction, language and physical movement without the production of physical objects, Sehgal insists that the "situations" must be presented continually during the museum's operating hours. His works can be bought and sold, and, by virtue of being repeatable, they can endure over time. But when selling his work, Sehgal stipulates that nothing may be written down; no catalog, no photos, no contract, no written receipt.

One of the most interesting aspects of Sehgal's work is his stated attempt to redefine art as "the transformation of actions rather than things." On the occasion of his creations, he wonders if something that is not an inanimate object can be considered valuable. He does not consider his work to be "performance" and he is insistent that it takes place in the context of a museum rather than a theater. In an establishment that places value on objects, he offers an alternative. He organizes the framework in which aliveness and interrelatedness between people can exist. He creates situations in which singular, ephemeral interactions might occur.

While museums and galleries generally place value upon objects, both commercial and not-for-profit theaters increasingly value marquee-named actors and flashy spectacle over aliveness and interrelatedness. For the generally hefty price of a ticket, you enter the sanctuary to witness technical virtuosity, brand-name actors and flashy stagecraft. But in order not to get lost in the visual and aural noise so prevalent in our times, perhaps it is necessary to regularly return to the essence and heartbeat of the theater: the creative relationship between the audience members and the actors.

Similar to musicians who intermittently revert to acoustic sessions or Dogme filmmakers who put strict limits on their methods, banishing elaborate special effects and technology, the theater can also return to its analog and unplugged origins. The core strength of the theater is that it is ultimately ephemeral and temporary. Existing only in the time set aside for its occasion, the theater event is dependent upon the mutual sensitivity, intelligence, flexibility and adventurousness of the assembled.

Not long after the cataclysmic events of 9/11, I launched a series of one-on-one conversations with various artists and theater people whom I admired. Open to the general public, the talks took place within the small 17-by-35-foot rectangle of the SITI Company studio in midtown Manhattan. I did not know that these conversations would fulfill a palpable need for substantive discussion in a room with no separation between the audience and the speakers. We all sat in the same light, breathed the same air and followed thoughts as they developed through the art of conversation. The event was, for lack of a better word, "acoustic" or "unplugged." Nothing in the presentation was enhanced or amplified in any sense of the word. Spectacle played no role in the conversations. The heat of human contact governed the experience.

In challenging times, spectacle takes the back seat in favor of the human need for intimacy and exchange. The post 9/11 days were already too saturated by spectacle and display. The constant replay of planes flying into buildings and people falling to their deaths, so reminiscent of action films, felt numbing and hallucinogenic. The "acoustic" encounters that became known as *Conversations with Anne* (now published by TCG as a book of the same name) provided an alternative to the dominant culture of spectacle. We gathered together in the charged space of conversation and encounter.

I crave aliveness. I want to be challenged and feel present, participatory and part of the conversation. I long for adventure and the charged atmosphere of stimulating encounters. But what is aliveness really? What constitutes a real meeting beyond the habitual co-existence with others or the mediated relationships of social networking? When does an authentic encounter begin?

Solitary confinement is known to be the worst prison sentence because isolation can cause serious damage to one's mental health. We find meaning in our relations with others. Without meaning we tend to give up and fall into repetitive patterns. And it is this search for meaning that keeps us from living in fear. The key to a healthy life is not to be alone, to breathe the same air with others, to share the sensation of living through moments together. But it is possible to live with people and still be fearful. It is possible to be isolated in the prison of one's own daily life. The senses shut down, we live in fear and resentment and routine replaces living. We start the process of closing down and hardening that leads to death.

In 1972, Polish theater director Jerzy Grotowski published a manifesto entitled *Holiday*, which ushered in what became known as his paratheatrical phase. He began to distance himself from the conventional theater, and he attempted instead to transcend the separation between audience and actors. Rather than spectacle, he was interested in the potential for human co-presence and exchange within a specific context. The word *holiday* is a translation from the Polish "swieto." Rather than vacation or time off work, "swieto" refers to the notion of the exceptional, the holy, sacred or special. Perhaps, closer to "holy day." In *Holiday* Grotowski introduced his vision of "active culture," a field in which participants, rather than creating new productions, worked towards co-creating encounters exemplified by "collective effervescence."

It is not theater that is indispensable but: to cross the frontiers between you and me; to come forward to meet you, so that we do not get lost in the crowd – or among words or in declarations, or among the beautifully precise thoughts.

(Jerzy Grotowski, theater director)

Generally, I gravitate towards a theater that speaks through metaphor. For me, the problem with the paratheatrical impulse is its propensity to abandon metaphor for direct experience. And yet what binds both the theater and the paratheatrical experiences seems to be the eternal human search for meaning. Without meaning we fall into repetitive patterns. Whether between actors or between actor and audience, what does it *mean* to approach one another in a pure sense? The meaning emerges in the encounter.

Getting better

The playwright Edward Albee insisted that only after he wrote 50 plays did his 51st become what he considers to be his first play. That much practice and that much writing had to occur before he could produce a truly original work. Two bestselling books, Malcolm Gladwell's *Outliers* and Daniel Coyle's *The Talent Code*, are popularizing neuroscience's revelation that 10,000 hours of practice is required before real innovation is possible.

Practice is action. Every skill developed is a form of memory constructed with practice. When I practice I am building reliable circuits. I am paying attention to errors and fixing them. I am breaking down a skill into component parts and repeating each action involved in that skill. The systemic firing of signals that happens when I practice deeply builds the high-speed circuits needed for the creative act.

I've got to admit it's getting better. It's a little better all the time.

(Paul McCartney, musician, songwriter)

Ellen Lauren traveled to Japan to perform and tour *King Lear* with Tadashi Suzuki's SCOT Company. "You must be exhausted," I pronounced upon her return. "No," she replied. "I feel invigorated by the experience." Despite the intensive travel, schedule, rehearsals, training and performance she felt energized by the perseverance and joy of the SCOT Company actors. According to Ellen, the actors relish the challenges of performance and the day-to-day maintenance of the company as well as what they call "self-rehearsals" where they toil alone in a studio, practicing and rehearsing. Despite the schedule and constant hard work, the actors are happy, explained Ellen, because, through the daily trials, they are getting better.

Perhaps it is human folly and irrationality in the face of the realities of the world – the violence, pestilence, decay and the innumerable insurmountable obstacles that we encounter every day – to persist in hoping for improvement. And yet, in the face of entropy, resistance and what can seem like the futility of any action in the world, "getting better" does sustain. We are not getting better simply for our own ends and gratification; rather, we are striving to get better in order to be more useful and connected to the world.

When I was a little girl, perhaps 11 or 12 years of age, I joined a competitive swim team on the Naval base in Norfolk, Virginia. Never particularly talented at sports, I was a terrible swimmer and came in last or close to last in each heat. However, our coach, a small, squat, bald man named Mr. Butt, inspired me to swim as hard and as fast as I possibly could. Each day after swim practice, I arrived home to eat leftovers from the family dinner and to squeeze in my school homework before going to bed exhausted. Inspired by Mr. Butt's words of encouragement and his belief in us, I dreamt of personally swimming in the Olympics. I returned to swim practice every day after school with renewed vigor and hopes for improvement.

Mr. Butt died unexpectedly, I believe from a heart attack. Shattered, I sat with the swim team at his funeral in a Catholic church. A week later the training resumed and Mr. Butt's daughter took over as coach. But without Mr. Butt's gruff brand of encouragement and inspiration, nothing was the same for me. One evening in front of the entire swim team, the new coach picked me out for ridicule. I do not remember her exact words but I do recall the sting, the smart, the insult, the embarrassment and the disappointment. She did not understand why I continued to train, pointing out that I was the one who always finished last. I did not remain on the team for even another day. I abandoned my dreams for improvement in swimming and for competition in the Olympics.

Support and encouragement are vital in the recipe for "getting better." Happily I continued to find arenas in which I felt encouraged and challenged to strive and to "get better." I trained and rode show horses for much of my adolescence. I spent years studying martial arts and foreign languages. Theater directing has always been a rigorous taskmaster that demands constant study and renewed discipline. The raw exposure of effort and practice has steadily allowed me to shed habit and renew my connection to the present moment.

For their class projects at Columbia University, the graduate directing students generally cast freelance New York City actors. Despite lack of remuneration, these actors, who have chosen the theater as their métier and New York as their springboard, make the journey at their own expense to the Upper Upper West Side to rehearse and perform with the directors-in-training. The directors often worry about asking too much of these generous actors. How dare they demand high levels of achievement for class projects and no money? One day during a notes session, one of the directors pointed out with great excitement that he finally understood that the actors chose to work with them because the projects offer them the opportunity to improve their craft, to *get better*. Finally the director felt that he could ask for the very best work from these actors at all times.

When I began to direct, I entered rooms with people I barely knew and tried to construct performances for audiences. I fell down and stood up and fell down and stood up and fell down again. The hours and hours of practice became the foundation for a life in the theater. Little by little I learned about the benefits of deep practice. I know that when I stop practicing I will stop transforming.

Chapter 3

Error

The main interest in life and work is to become someone else that you were not in the beginning.

(Michel Foucault, philosopher, social theorist)

As an undergraduate at Bard College in 1972 I joined Via Theater, a company launched by classmate Ossian Cameron, in order to investigate Jerzy Grotowski's book *Towards a Poor Theater*. Every weekday morning from 8 to 10, in the basement of an abandoned dining hall, we shared rigorous physical training; and in the evenings we rehearsed plays in what we imagined to be the manner of the book. From what we understood, Grotowski's approach eliminated scenery, costumes and special effects in order to place the actor, unencumbered and vulnerable, in direct, unmediated relation to the audience. We often traveled together from Bard to New York and other cities to experience the radical new innovations of Joseph Chaikin and the Open Theater, Richard Schechner's Performance Group (an earlier manifestation of the Wooster Group), Peter Brook's International Centre for Theatre Research, Jerzy Grotowski's Theatre Laboratory and Richard Foreman's Ontological-Hysteric Theater. These journeys were exciting and formative and gave us a taste of the vibrant theater scene happening during those years.

After seeing Richard Foreman's production *Dr. Selavy's Magic Theater* at the Mercer Arts Center in Manhattan I formed the I Hate Richard Foreman Club, an alliance of like-minded colleagues who despised the theater made by director Richard Foreman. To us, Foreman's theater seemed the antithesis of everything that we believed in so passionately. We felt that he treated his actors like mindless mannequins who had no autonomy or creative role to play in the rehearsal process. We called his theater trickery and intellectualism.

In the spring of 1973 we learned that Bard had invited Foreman to speak to film students. The I Hate Richard Foreman Club leapt into action. We planned to attend the talk and make our attack. As it turned out, no film students showed up for Foreman's presentation. This did not prevent us from speaking up. "You treat your actors like props," we accused him. "Yes," he responded evenly. "You have no respect for actors," we continued. He did not seem at all ruffled. He left us alone to watch a video of his play Sophia = Wisdom saying that he did not enjoy seeing his work on tape. We sat through the screening more enraged than ever.

In 1974, after graduating from Bard, I moved to New York City and for a while lived in Soho, one block away from Foreman's Ontological-Hysteric Theater. At the time his rehearsals were open to visitors. Whenever I had a free night I visited Foreman's rehearsal or watched a performance. Inevitably I would exit fuming and irritable, telling everyone I knew how much I hated Richard Foreman's work. Then the next free evening, wondering what to do, I would once again find myself at the Ontological-Hysteric Theater.

This charade lasted for about a year until I suddenly realized that I had learned more from Foreman's plays and rehearsals than from any other theater artist. The I Hate Richard Foreman Club had been, in fact, a mistake. I had been in error. And then I recognized the depth of Richard Foreman's influence upon me. The performances and the psychic environments of his productions are aggressive and yet rigorous, and he seemed never to disguise problems. The plays are jagged and radical, never gentle, and they perceptually challenge audiences to wake up. Just as you get into the groove, the interruptions stir you up. Foreman consciously places obstacles, often string or Plexiglas, between the audience and the actors and inserts interruptions of loud sound and blinding light. With such distancing or alienation effects, I wondered if Foreman might be Bertolt Brecht's closest aesthetic descendent. Over the intervening years, Foreman's work has continued to kick me in the head: from Hotel for Criminals to Rhoda in Potato-land, from Pandering to the Masses to Egyptology, he taught me about how human perception can be chronicled theatrically, using the languages of the stage. And by examples found in his work, Foreman showed me how consciously exposing human error is inherently theatrical.

Years later I told the story about the I Hate Richard Foreman Club to lighting designer Heather Carson, who often works with Foreman. Carson told Foreman, who was characteristically delighted. During technical rehearsals he would implore, "Oh, Heather, tell the 'I Hate Richard Foreman Club' story again."

It is only through frustration that conscience comes into play, and man transcends a slothful animal state.

(Richard Foreman, theater director)

Most significant growth in my life has been the direct result of errors, mistakes, accidents, faulty assumptions and wrong moves. I have generally learned more from my mistakes and my so-called failures than any successes or instances of "being right." I would venture to propose that this equation is also true in the world at large. Error is a powerful animating ingredient in political, scientific and historical evolution as well as in art and mythology. Error is a necessity. The question I had to ask myself was: how can I cultivate a tolerance and an appetite for being wrong, for error?

In the face of an exceedingly complicated world, there are too many people who are invested in "being right." These people are dangerous. Their authority is based upon their sense of certainty. But innovation and invention do not only happen with smart people who have all of the answers. Innovation results from trial and error. The task is to make good mistakes, good errors, in the right direction.

There are many reasons that we get things as wrong as often as we do. Failures of perception, the cause of most error, are far more common in our daily lives than we like to think. We make errors because of inattention, because of poor preparation and because of haste. We err as a result of hardened prejudices about how things are. We err because we neglect to think things through. Our senses betray us constantly. But the chaos caused by being wrong also awakens energy and consciousness in us. In the moments that we realize our faults of perception, we are jerked into an awareness of our humanity. The Slovenian philosopher Slavoj Žižek wrote, "Consciousness originates with something going terribly wrong."

The concrete meaning of the Latin word *error* is to "wander about" or "stray." In rehearsal, when things go wrong, when things fall apart, my job as the director is to stay present and resist concretization as long as I can. I try to consciously allow for error, for wandering, in order to progress towards something fruitful.

Being wrong rarely feels good. It is natural to feel mortified by the mistakes that we make. Admitting that one is wrong, admitting to making an error can be annoying, even humiliating. The awkward struggles and embarrassment resulting from error are part of what makes us human. But without error, very little progress is possible. The question is, how to welcome being wrong as a necessary part of the creative process.

Error is a problem that demands adjustment. As I mentioned in Chapter 2, Pablo Picasso proposed that the first stroke on the blank canvas is *always* a mistake and the rest of the work on the canvas is to fix that mistake. The action of adjustment and correction is where creative expression starts. Adam and Eve ate the infamous apple, an enormous mistake – an error. The blunder catapulted them both into the new, harsh world that we mortals inherited and inhabit today. A play normally begins when something goes wrong, when the pendulum swings wide, when imbalance rules and thereby the drama develops. Characters struggle to regain balance and harmony from a state of imbalance, wrongness and error, and these are the struggles that stimulate pathos and empathy in the audience.

Our capacity to tolerate error depends upon our capacity to tolerate emotion.

(Irna Gadd, clinical social worker)

In 1974 I moved to New York City with the dream of making a life in the theater but first I had to find gainful employment to support my passions. Here are some of my many day jobs: collecting overdue payments from the clients of a bottled water company; teaching theater to adolescents at the United Nations International School after-school program; analyzing expenses for a Wall Street brokerage firm; and leading theater workshops in a halfway house for schizophrenics. Each job provided a window into a particular social, political or economic world. Each window taught me valuable lessons about how to be a better theater director. I mostly learned through the errors that I brought to these jobs based upon my faulty assumptions. After many, many mistakes, I eventually learned to abandon my own carefully premeditated plans, to slow down and listen, really listen to what was happening, and then to adjust. I learned the necessity of giving up control in order to ride the wave that was already in motion.

Hired to lead theater workshops at the Postgraduate Center for Mental Health, a halfway house in midtown Manhattan, my initial plan was to guide the clients, as the mental-health patients were called, through my own brand of rigorous physical theater. The Postgraduate Center for Mental Health served a community generally not dysfunctional enough to be hospitalized but also not well enough to be out on the streets. My workshop was one of the panoply of daily activities offered to them, including group therapy, book clubs and cooking classes. Thinking that it would be useful and therapeutic for the participants to sweat, I carefully devised rigorous movement and trust exercises that would demand extroversion and attention to one another. On the very first day of the workshop, eight clients showed up eager to participate. I introduced the exercises I had so carefully prepared only to discover that they absolutely hated them. Sweating for no apparent reason was of no interest whatsoever to any of them. By the next week only four people showed up for the class and the following week, two. In despair, I finally asked the two remaining participants to help me out. "What do you want to do?" I asked, to which they replied without hesitation, "Musical comedy." "Well, OK," I said. "I do not know anything about musical comedy, so why not show me what musical comedy is." The two remaining participants stood up and performed a few bits of songs and comic dialogue. Word got around the center quickly. The following week six participants materialized, excited about doing musical comedy improvisations, and I continued to follow their lead. A week later word had spread further about the musical comedy workshop and 15 participants showed up. The escalation continued and more and more clients arrived every week. When the workshop surpassed 50 participants, we had to move into a much larger space.

The room into which I walked for each workshop was a perfect description of chaos and beyond anything I could imagine or, much less, control. Leading the workshop became an exercise in juggling countless diverse bits of information and stimuli simultaneously and keeping things moving. The vision before me as I entered the room was always arresting: someone playing Gershwin or Chopin on an upright piano, others lying on gymnastic mats fast asleep, someone reading aloud while rocking back and forth, a reckless tango rehearsal, a spitting argument, a budding romance and so on. Anything was possible. Once the session got underway, I never knew from one moment to the next who might walk onstage and sing an aria or launch into a monologue or introduce a new character or sing a duet. Clients wandered in and out of the room and into and out of the improvisations fluidly. My job was to pilot the rollercoaster. I was the one who sweated during these sessions. Every ounce of my attention, quick thinking and responsiveness was required. At each and every moment I had to be able to either stop someone from getting hurt, encourage a shy person to participate, laugh, shout, applaud or jump into the fray myself. I needed to be able to adjust, at any millisecond, to the constantly altering environment.

Working at the Postgraduate Center for Mental Health was probably the best director training imaginable. None of my carefully crafted plans could ever be sufficient to deal with the pandemonium unleashed during each session. Eventually I learned to welcome moments that seemed out of my control, too chaotic or outside the range of my experience and accept that this is precisely when the world opens outwards to reveal a reality far larger and richer than anything that I could imagine or premeditate.

Chaos should be regarded as extremely good news.
(Trungpa Rinpoche, Buddhist meditation master)

Errors, accidents and chaos can be creative partners, even guides, informing and assisting the artistic process. In an interview about his working process, the American film director Robert Altman said, "Think about five of your favorite moments in any of my films and I can guarantee that they were accidents." His method was to gather a crew, invite his favorite actors on location and allow the errors and disorder to commence.

The question is, how to relax in the face of trouble and strife and remain capable of seeing what is happening and then what happens after that? I start by recognizing the precise moment when my resistance to the unfamiliar arises. Where exactly does my tolerance break down? Where are my boundaries? In that moment, rather than stop or withdraw, I try to open up, feel and then move. I try to keep moving.

Chaos, in biblical usage, is a chasm or abyss. For an artist it feels like disorder, unpredictability or confusion. We all have our boundaries and our limits of tolerance. But in order to be engaged in the artistic process, which is a form of action in the world, it is necessary to allow some degree of chaos and error into the process and into our perceptions. Is it possible to tease out the limits of what is tolerable? Can chance be part of the process? How much control is necessary?

Our resistance to error is, in no small part, a resistance to being left alone with too few certainties and too many emotions.
(Kathryn Schulz, journalist, writer)

I am by nature a controlling person, which probably has something to do with why I became a director. I wanted to create a tolerable environment, the rehearsal hall, in the midst of what I felt to be a relatively hostile and intolerable world. For a director it is typically difficult to welcome accidents, chaos and error into rehearsal because it is so difficult to give up control. Much of my job is to be decisive, to propose solutions, to demand a certain quality of attention, to set the staging and to edit ideas. I know that without sufficient order, specificity and detail, the stage picture will suffer. But I also know that with too much order and no room for accidents or spontaneity, the production will lack life and energy.

In 1998 I had the opportunity to see my own work in performance in a way that was far more chaotic than I had originally planned or envisaged. And based upon that experience, to this day I strive to allow for a little more chaos and error into every project.

As part of a trilogy of plays based on the roots of American popular entertainment, *American Silents* was about the genesis of film and the art of acting for silent films. The other two parts of the trilogy were *American Vaudeville*, about the great American art form of vaudeville that flourished between 1840 and 1920, and *Marathon Dancing*, a music-theater piece that traced the American spirit of endurance in the intense events of month-long dance contests.

I directed *American Silents* with graduate acting students at Columbia University. The play was staged on a large sound stage on 42nd Street and 10th Avenue. Inspired by the earlier spatial symphonies of Luca Ronconi (*Orlando Furioso*) and Robert Wilson (*The $ Value of Man*), I envisioned the first half hour of the show as a promenade for the audience. The sound stage was divided into many smaller compartments, much like the studios where silent films were shot in the early part of the twentieth century. The audience was encouraged to wander freely from one tiny studio to another to observe the actors, directors and camera crew, all simultaneously at work on different film projects. At the end of the half hour of roaming freely amidst the cacophony, true to the silent-film stages of the time, bells rang and the crew manually deconstructed the compartments, transforming the stage into a large open space. Meanwhile, the audience was escorted to the bleachers upon which they watched the remainder of the play.

In order to stage the promenade section of the play, I rehearsed with each constellation of actors separately in the different compartments in order to create a precisely choreographed and timed scene that showed the photographing of a different silent film. I took great care of the clarity of the staging and the spatial and temporal composition of each of the 12 scenes separately. Ultimately all the scenes happened simultaneously as the audience walked around and observed.

In previews and on the opening night, the audience appeared quite interested in the promenade aspect of the performance, wandering around the theater, looking at each of the scenes as if set free on a silent-film stage. When the bells rang they also seemed happy to find seating on the bleachers to observe the remainder of the show in a more traditional manner. Everything worked as planned. Following the premiere I left New York for two weeks to work on another project but returned for the closing night of *American Silents*. But this evening the audience behaved quite differently. Early on, a few people spied the bleachers and sat down prematurely. With a crowd sensibility, the remaining audience followed suit and soon the entire audience had seated themselves on the bleachers ten minutes earlier than planned. In great despair about the failure of the idea, there was nothing for me to do but join the audience. I sat down sheepishly only to finally look up towards the stage to see an extraordinary spectacle that I never had the wit, talent or ability to stage. From the distance of the bleachers, the wide spectrum of movement and chaos felt like a *real* sound studio. The scenes were not coordinated or controlled. And yet the space was brimming with a kind of chaotic and glorious life that one can only find in real life. Each of the carefully composed compositions clashed with the other. I loved it and relished the extraordinary symphony of movement and sound and cacophony. How could I work intentionally to create work that has the scale, complexity and even chaos that I saw before me? I knew that the key to the answer of this question lay in my capacity to tolerate error.

Fallor ergo sum (I err, therefore I am).

(St. Augustine, Christian theologian)

Becoming conscious of error is how we learn and how we change. Our mistakes can teach us who we are because the capacity to err is central to human development. In the midst of the realization that we are wrong, we transform our understanding of ourselves as well as our ideas about the world. But we live in a culture that simply does not value error enough.

I have learned through my own mistakes that the only way to safeguard against error is to embrace it. I have also recognized the necessity to step outside my desire to feel right because I know that being wrong is crucial to my development as an artist. If I could freeze the frame on each of my mistakes, what I would see would be change, and in that moment, in the midst of my realization of error, progress begins.

Chapter 4

Limits

Art is a process and a journey. All artists have to find ways to lie to themselves, find ways to fool themselves into believing that what they're doing is good enough, the best they can do at that moment, and that's okay. Every work of art falls short of what the artist envisioned. It is precisely that gap between their intention and their execution that opens up the door for the next work.

(Eric Fischl, visual artist)

I transferred to Bard College in January of 1972, the fourth and final undergraduate institution that I attended. At registration I announced loudly that I wanted to study directing and was told that I would have to take a course in acting instead; I was assigned to a class taught by an elderly gentleman in a natty suit named Neil McKenzie. The class seemed quite close-knit and I was clearly the outsider joining in to their process. As I entered the studio on the first day, everyone was already in place and I stood awkwardly in front of the class. "What do you want to learn here, Bubbeleh?" asked Mr. McKenzie, who tended to call all of his students "Bubbeleh." Cornered, I answered, "I want to learn about different styles of acting." Mr. McKenzie looked at me sternly and said, "We do not study styles here; rather, we study acting." I was embarrassed and put in my place.

Over the years I have understood that Mr. McKenzie was correct. Style is determined after the fact. Style is a byproduct of the intensity, compression, objectivity, subjectivity, sustained attention, gathering, ruminating, eliminating, arranging and finally expression of the artistic process. Style is an inevitable consequence of this activity in concert with the limitations confronted in the process. To start with too much interest in style, I believe, is a mistake.

Johnny Cash once said, "Your style is a function of your limitations, more so than a function of your skills." According to some musicologists, what gives the specific style or sound to the Rolling Stones is that Mick

Jagger and Keith Richards are as close to singing "wrongly" or off-pitch as achievable without becoming unbearably off-key to the listener. And this "wrongness" or nuance is what creates their particular recognizable style. These days the music industry corrects singers' pitches technologically with software designed to smooth out any off-key notes in a singer's vocal track. This software would wreck the particular sound that makes the Rolling Stones so singular and attractive.

If style is indeed a result of given limits, it is best determined after the event.

Young artists often look to forge a personal signature. But ultimately a personal signature evolves from the constant renewal of attempts, a return to the drawing board, rather than an enforced, imposed style. Perhaps the ubiquitous corporate, consumer culture encourages artists to obsess about their style and the development of a brand. In the light of this pressure, I try instead to concentrate on the immersion, the process and the attention to craft, all of which eventually reveal styles that I could never have imagined before.

I have had the pleasure of encountering several mature artists who seem to have completely transcended style. So many styles had appeared and disappeared, materialized and passed through them, that these individuals seemed to be simply present in the moment. The late cellist and conductor Mstislav Rostropovich, for example, who lived a life so filled with music that by the time I met him late in his life he seemed like a child, open to the vicissitudes of the world around him. It seemed to me that he had channeled so much music through his body that he simply became a living conduit for the music that moved through him. He held on to nothing. The very best artists pass through countless styles. As fast as their audiences generate names and methods for their output, these groundbreaking artists switch the game. They simply let go. Examine the life trajectories of Pablo Picasso or Willem de Kooning or the careers of Constantin Stanislavsky or Jerzy Grotowski.

> But art is not technology; it is useless but vital. It is through art that we communicate what it feels like to be alive. When you ask "what is the point of art?" you could reformulate the question to "what is the point of human beings?"
>
> (Anthony Gormley, visual artist)

Towards the end of my undergraduate studies at Bard College, one of my professors, Roberta Sklar, who had worked extensively with Joseph Chaikin and the Open Theater, offered me the following advice: "Go to New York, find a writer and form a company." I valued her opinion. I moved to New York City in 1974, into a loft space on Grand Street between Broadway and Crosby Streets in Soho, before the neighborhood became the expensive shopping district that it is today. During the day-time, Soho was crowded with trucks loading and unloading cargo from the factories and storage spaces that are now today's expensive living lofts and retail stores. My loft had three bedrooms, a living room, dining room, kitchen and a sizable dance studio. The entire rent: $325 per month. Lack of heat was the only drawback. I shared the space with two dancers and we froze through the winter months, each paying only a little over $100 per month rent. I found a job in the collections department of a company that sold water coolers. This was the first of my many non-theater jobs in New York City. But in my mind I kept hearing Roberta Sklar's words: "Find yourself a writer and form a company."

I asked every New York theater person that I met, "How do you find actors?" Most advised me to put an ad in *Backstage*, a weekly newspaper that published casting notices, resources and articles of interest to actors. And so I wrote an ad: "Looking for actors interested in an investigation of assassination and murder using Shakespeare's *Macbeth*." I submitted it in person to the *Backstage* offices. *Showbiz*, another weekly actor's periodical of the time, must have liked the ad because they included it in their own publication for free.

And then my phone began to ring. Incessantly. To this day I shudder at the sound of an analog telephone. Hundreds of actors called me to ask about the ad. Half of the actors hung up when I said "no money," a detail that I had neglected to include in the *Backstage* ad. The other half wanted to audition.

Frightened by the prospect of auditions with real New York City actors, I decided to hold interviews instead, inviting one person at a time to the loft on Grand Street. I sat behind a table in the dance studio, shaking with terror. My hands trembled so I sat bolt upright, clutching the edge of the table so that no one could see how acutely nervous I was. In addition to an interview I asked each actor to read from a poem by Sylvia Plath entitled *Cut*.

One of the scores of actors who came for an interview, a man at least twice my age whose breath smelled of alcohol, made an impression upon me that has lasted until this day. His substantial résumé included film, TV, Broadway, Off Broadway, Off Off Broadway and commercials. We spoke at length. At the end of our interview he burst into tears, "I just want to do something meaningful."

Thrown off by a grown man crying and touched by his wish to work with a young director like me who had little experience and no money, the auditions gave me insight into the plight of the actor in the American theater system. I had opened the lid of Pandora's box and what I encountered there forced me to re-examine all of the assumptions I had accumulated about actors, the actor–director relationship and the circumstances of an actor's day-to-day existence. Up until that moment I selfishly assumed that actors were judging me, seeing through me into my own insecurities. I made the situation about me. The experience gave me a deep empathy and lasting appreciation for actors.

We are pawns in a game whose forces we largely fail to comprehend. We usually think of ourselves sitting in the driver's seat, with ultimate control over the decisions we make and the direction our life takes; but, alas, this perception has more to do with our desires – and with how we want to view ourselves – than with reality.

(Dan Ariely, psychologist)

Working in the cradle of the downtown New York theater scene of the late 1970s and early 1980s, I was accustomed to working with very little to create the productions that launched my career. I was accustomed to limits. With no budget and no support, not to mention no actual theater spaces, I began to work with like-minded colleagues and together we created productions on rooftops and in shop windows, in abandoned schoolhouses and even once in abandoned detective offices.

In my early years in New York City I made pilgrimages to many small Off Off Broadway theaters hoping to direct a play in a legitimate theatrical venue. Due to my inexperience and slim résumé, most places turned me away. Not to be undone, I managed to create theater anyway, in non-theatrical spaces. Finally luck seemed to strike when I met George Bartenieff, co-artistic director at the time with his wife, Chrystal Field, of Theater for the New City on 10th Street and First Ave. Sympathetic and interested, Bartenieff mentioned that he and his wife were considering turning their prop room into a theater. "It is a very small space but I see no reason why you might not do something in there." Thrilled by the breakthrough, a gig in a genuine New York theater venue, I could not wait to report the good news to the four actors I was working with. All of us were encouraged and excited, and so in anticipation of our legitimate theater and New York debut we rehearsed wherever we could, sometimes in church basements, friends' living spaces and often in my home. By this time, I was living in a brownstone in the Fort Greene section of Brooklyn long before that area's eventual gentrification. I shared the rent for an entire three-story house, $325 per month, with David Schechter, a friend from my Bard days who was performing at the time on Broadway in Liz Swados's musical, *Runaways*.

A week before we were scheduled to premiere, I returned to Theater for the New City to remind Bartenieff that we would be showing up to take over the theater's prop room. When he saw me coming I saw his eyes cloud over. Clearly embarrassed, he said, "Oh, Chrystal decided that she does not want to turn the prop room into a theater. Sorry." He shrugged his shoulders and I left in the depths of despair. When I reported this new development to the actors, one of the four quit. Fortunately, the other three were as determined as I to continue with the project. But the question lingered, where were we to perform?

David Schechter suggested that we transform our house into a theater. "We have plenty of room for an audience," he said. At first I resisted. Who would come to Brooklyn to see a play? These were the days before Brooklyn became a coveted destination. But with no other option, I gave in and began to figure out how to address the practical challenges of doing a play in a house in an obscure neighborhood in the Borough of Brooklyn.

A friend owned a truck and offered to transport the audience every night from Manhattan to Brooklyn. We decided to call our play *Inhabitat* and I put a tiny ad in *The Village Voice* instructing audiences to meet on the corner of LaGuardia Place and Third Street in Manhattan. We could fit exactly 27 people into the truck and into the various rooms of the house. Because the truck was windowless, the audience had no idea where they were headed or even that they were crossing the Manhattan Bridge into the heart of Brooklyn. As the audience climbed out of the truck they found themselves in front of the brownstone on shabby Fort Greene Place. Didi O'Connell, playing a character named Fanny, stood at the top of the steps at the front door of the house in a puffy ski jacket, carrying a bulging bag of groceries under each arm. She spoke the first monologue directly to the audience, then turned to enter the house. The audience followed and moved freely through the various rooms, privy to our carefully staged domestic scenes. The three actors spoke text sampled freely from plays by Pinter, Beckett, Chekhov and other writers. At the end of the play the entire audience gathered in the large kitchen-dining room for the final scene.

One night, to my surprise and glee, the composer John Cage attended *Inhabitat* and was thoroughly delighted. "The sound of the dogs barking outside," he said, "mixed wonderfully with the scenes indoors." Cage told everyone he knew about the show, which I am sure helped it to became a minor cult hit in the downtown scene. Because of *Inhabitat*, I became known for working in found spaces or what later became known as "site-specific theater." The irony was that I dreamed of directing a play in a real theater. I did not even like the sound of the dogs barking outside the house. Nevertheless, with no obvious alternative, I continued directing plays in non-theatrical environments.

In retrospect, each project did teach me how to work with architecture, with weather, with hardship and with limitations, and it provided an excellent training ground in design, producing, audience management and composition. The challenges and limitations of site-specific productions also offered the opportunity to work with sets that would be cost prohibitive inside of a theater: large building fronts, abandoned schoolhouses, a construction site with the backdrop view of the Twin Towers of the World Trade Center and other challenging environments. The limitations that I faced seem to be exactly what I needed then in order to learn how to direct theater.

Limitations are what I push up against and the pushing is what ultimately makes me stronger and more resilient. Obstacles and limitations demand concomitant energy to confront them. Without energy, art is weak-kneed. The bigger the obstacles and limitations, the more will and energy are needed to confront them. If I had obtained what I wanted right away, in this case a real theater, if I had not had to become creative with very little means, it would have taken me much longer to progress.

> We may have a perfectly adequate way of doing something, but that does not mean there cannot be a better way. So we set out to find an alternative way. This is the basis of any improvement that is not fault correction or problem solving.
>
> (Edward de Bono, physician, consultant)

I invited actors and collaborators at the start of each new project to brainstorm ideas together. I called the brainstorming sessions *lateral thinking*. Inspired by Edward de Bono's 1970 book of the same name, *lateral thinking* is a method of collective cross-referential, non-judgmental, collaborative thinking that teaches how to move from vertical, goal-oriented, egoist thinking to lateral cooperative thinking. The point of the exercise was not to imagine something and then have it materialize. What mattered was how the lateral thinking interfaced with the actual four-dimensional world of limitations and obstacles. For example, we imagined a pack of motorcycles that would arrive at the beginning of the third act of *Out of Sync*, our adaptation of Chekhov's *Seagull* set in Manhattan's East Village. We did not ultimately succeed in finding a motorcycle gang willing to show up every night for the show. We ended up with a lone bicycle. But, due to our process of lateral thinking, the presence of the bicycle had weight, necessity and meaning. The budgetary and practical limitations required us to transform the motorcycle gang into another solution. When we finally settled on a bicycle, we all understood why it was there, its dramaturgical function, and we knew how to use it in the play.

At first it's not possible to describe anything beyond a wish or a desire. That's how it begins, making a film, writing a book, painting a picture, composing a tune, generally creating something. You have a wish. You wish that something might exist, and often, you work on it until it does. You want to give something to the world, something truer, more beautiful, more painstaking, more serviceable, or simply something other than what already exists. And right at the start, simultaneous with the wish, you imagine what that something other might be like, or at least you see something flash by. And then you set off in the direction of the flash, and you hope you don't lose your orientation, or forget the wish.

(Wim Wenders, filmmaker)

I unexpectedly ran into trouble in the *absence* of limitations and obstacles. Hired to direct the graduating actors from the acting academy in West Berlin in 1981, I proposed a devised work about Berlin that I would create with the actors. At my first meeting with the German designers I proceeded to conduct a lateral thinking session, as I was accustomed to doing in the New York downtown no-budget productions. Lots of exciting ideas emerged. I proposed that the audience would spend the first part of the production in promenade around the theater building. Using the terminology from medieval times, I suggested that we would build a series of *mansions*. In medieval theater *mansions* were small stages representing heaven, hell or purgatory, and the audience would move, as in a church, from mansion to mansion, watching the repeated performances. I suggested that one of the mansions could be a peepshow complete with windows for the audience to look through with an actress positioned upon a rotating disc at the center of the peepshow. To my horror, the designers and the crew built exactly what I described. I came into the scene shop one day to find a life-size peepshow. And so it continued. The German team built everything that I described at our first meeting. The resulting production was not at all good because it lacked the necessary process of difficulty, adjustment, pressure, compression and re-adjustment in light of limitations and obstacles. The process lacked development and resistance.

I depend upon the given constraints of any project because the limitations require me to be creative. The limits are what define the endeavor. Without limits, there is nothing to push against. Without limitations, I can only fail.

> You cannot go into the womb to form the child; it is there and makes itself and comes forth whole ... Of course you have a little more control over your writing than that; but let it take you and if it seems to take you off the track don't hold back.
>
> (Gertrude Stein, novelist)

Perhaps it is true that there are good Beginners, good Middlers and good Enders. And perhaps it is also true that no one person can be all three. I am a good Beginner and a good Middler but, left to unconscious habit, I am a lousy Ender. In the process of production, I relish the research, the preparation and the work with designers. I love the initial weeks of rehearsal. On the first day of rehearsal I am at my best conveying every idea and launching into the shared collaborative adventure. I love the engagement and pursuit, the hunt of the rehearsal process. But by the time we arrive at technical rehearsals I tend to run out of steam. I have more or less already moved on to the next project. Much to the general consternation of my team, I am already ablaze with ideas and excitement about the next project while we are still trying to fine-tune the one for which we are in tech. It is for this reason that I collaborate with people who are good Enders. The balance works out but I wonder about this tendency to weaken when the going gets critical.

Personally, I am surprised about how easily I give up towards the end of any endeavor. Whether the end of a rehearsal process or the end of a day or the end of a conversation, if I am not exceedingly vigilant, I tend to weaken towards the finish line. I notice that it starts in my body, in my muscles. As my muscles begin to weaken from physical exertion, I give up. I used to enjoy running out of doors. Whenever I approached whatever I had had determined as the finish line, rather than speed up and accelerate towards the conclusion, my body slowed down. My default proclivity is to lose steam towards the end.

Because I am familiar with my tendency to lose steam towards the end of a process, I have developed a vigilance concerning this predisposition. When confronted with the finish line I try to apply will, memory and discipline in the face of my slackening of energy. *Tapas* in Sanskrit means both discipline and heat. With resistance and then effort, heat is generated. Sometimes I cower before a problem only to find that actual engagement, *tapas*, generates the heat necessary to dissolve the obstacles.

Each of us was born with strengths, weaknesses and limitations. Our limits can drive us and can even determine our own particular style or method. I am naturally a bit slow and clumsy. And yet I love speed, grace and physical clarity. Perhaps my own choreographic approach to the theater is the result of my physical incompetence. I gravitate towards actors who can move through space in ways that I can only dream of doing personally.

The visual artist Chuck Close is seriously prosopagnosic, which means that he has grave difficulty recognizing faces, even of people he knows intimately. And he is obsessed with painting faces. By painting portraits he found that he is better able to recognize and remember faces. He said, "I was not conscious of making a decision to paint portraits because I have difficulty recognizing faces. That occurred to me 20 years after the fact when I looked at why I was still painting portraits, why that still had urgency for me. I began to realize that it has sustained me for so long because I have difficulty in recognizing faces." Although a catastrophic spinal artery collapse in 1988 left him severely paralyzed, Close has continued to paint and produce extraordinary portraits sought after by museums and collectors around the world.

Limits can also be consciously and methodically selected as a creative partner. In 1995, Danish film directors Lars von Trier and Thomas Vinterberg, in response to what they considered an over-the-top Hollywood film industry, initiated a movement that they called *Dogme*. Their goal was to purify filmmaking by refusing to use expensive special effects, post-production modifications or technical gimmicks. The Dogme adherents proposed that it is better to concentrate on the story and the actors' performances than distracting overproduction. They produced ten rules that were agreed upon by other filmmakers who worked within the Dogme limitations, which included: shooting only on location, no special lighting, no overdubbed music, only handheld cameras and using only the props and sets found on the site. Many noteworthy films were made using Dogme rules, referred to as the "vow of chastity," including: *The Idiots* by von Trier, *The Celebration* by Vinterberg, *Open Hearts* by Susanne Bier and *Julien Donkey-Boy* by Harmony Korine.

Once we accept our limits, we go beyond them.
(Albert Einstein, theoretical physicist)

As a girl I was obsessed with horses. My first paid job, at the age of 15, was to teach horseback riding at a stable in Rhode Island. I also had the great fortune to train two-year-old horses. I was accustomed to being thrown to the ground, but at the age of 20 a horse fell directly on top of me, causing tremendous stress and trauma to my hips and legs. As the years progressed, walking became increasingly painful. I mostly kept the pain to myself and whenever anyone asked me if I was limping I would vehemently shake my head "no" and then chastise myself for not exercising enough or working sufficiently on my alignment. Still in my twenties, an orthopedic surgeon suggested hip replacement but I was adamant about finding a less traumatic remedy.

At the end of June 2012, I finally had both hips replaced at the Hospital for Special Surgery in Manhattan. It required about two months to recuperate and to learn how to negotiate the world with large new pieces of metal inserted with great craft and skill into my hips and thighbones. At first my body reacted in shock, shooting fluids to hips, legs and feet, causing much swelling, which is a perfectly normal reaction to trauma. The body activated rescue measures as though I had been in a massive car accident. As the days progressed post-surgery, I confused my body even further by commencing physical therapy. Trying to move my swollen legs and feet, pushing with intent against the system's shock-protective mechanism caused what seemed to be even more physical confusion. The muscles, tendons and ligaments surrounding a total hip replacement require time to heal after surgery before they can once again provide stability to the ball and the socket. Little by little my body calmed down and adjusted to the altered landscape, and learned to accept and profit from the new circumstances. Neuroscience shows how the brain can adjust after trauma and learns to use the healthy fragments to do the job of other injured parts. It is clear that the human body, as part of the same ecosystem as the brain, also learns to use the situation at hand and utilize the available parts.

After leaving the hospital I spent one week at the Burke Rehabilitation Hospital near White Plains, New York, where every morning I was wheeled to a wing of the building to join what seemed like hundreds of other patients in wheelchairs for occupational and physical therapy. During the time in residence at Burke I felt as if I were in a Fellini film or perhaps a Thomas Mann novel. A sprawling series of buildings built around 1915 and surrounded by vast green lawns, Burke services patients with serious rehabilitation issues caused by all sorts of trauma. In the setting of the massive institution everyone has a job – to recover or to tend to those in recovery. Every patient had a story and all of us struggled together to regain movement and flexibility. From 9:30 till 4:30 each weekday we were wheeled from one physical or occupational therapy class to the next in order to learn how to function during the healing process and within the required restrictions and limitations, or what is called "precautions." Much like broken bones that are placed in slings or casts, these limitations on movement allow the body to accept and integrate the new hardware until the adaptation process is complete and the body is strong enough to continue with everyday living.

Director Robert Woodruff told me that during his recuperative period after spinal surgery he learned to enjoy what he called "the art of slow." I often remembered his words during my own recovery. The "art of slow" requires patience and an appreciation of the possible latitude and spaciousness within limitations. Learning to appreciate the "art of slow" was challenging. Within the set precautions that limited my "doing," it was possible to discover new layers of "being."

After Burke my beloved Rena drove me to our home in Manhattan, to begin the process of completing the necessary eight weeks of precautions. Rena cooked, cleaned, helped me put on and take off clothes, shower. Everything. Her consistent empathy with each and every step of my recovery never lagged. She experienced the ups and the downs *with* me. Her devotion was love in action and my own love for her deepened every day. I slept a lot. I watched seven seasons of *Monk* on Netflix. I moved religiously through the exacting prescribed PT exercises and attended physical therapy three times a week at the Hospital for Special Surgery.

The choreographer Molissa Fenley came to visit during my recuperation and with great compassion for my recovery process described a piece she choreographed on herself not long after her own ACL reconstruction surgery in which a section of her hamstring's tendon was stapled into place on either side of her knee. The tendon then required nine months to learn how to become a ligament. She was given a strict format of restrictions upon her movement possibilities. From these limitations she created a beautiful three-part dance entitled *Regions* made in accordance with the "menu" that she was given by her physical therapist towards a healing calendar. The first part, *Chair*, is performed in a chair because this is all that her limitations allowed. *Ocean Walk*, the second part, was made when she was allowed to walk forward but with no turning. She then made *Mesa*, the third and concluding part, when she was finally able to use almost all her skills but with minimal jumping. (See the entire dance on her website: www.molissafenley.com/video.php.)

While the alien bits of metal in my hips and legs searched for stability, I struggled to be patient, follow the PT's instructions and find grace in the situation. Learning the "art of slow" within the restraint of strict limitations, I tried to experience spaciousness and make unexpected discoveries. In Molissa Fenley's dances I see extension, magnetism and

great expressivity within the confines of her "menu of precautions."
I wondered what my own version of her expressivity might be?

Eventually the alien bits of metal in my hips and thighs became my
friends. Thanks to the intervention of surgery I found a complete recon-
nection with daily life, a happy reboot. During the enforced eight weeks of
stillness, adaptation and change, I did the best I could to be patient and
have faith in the process while adjusting to new limits.

Towards the end of his life, Merce Cunningham performed in public
sitting in a chair. Despite the minimal nature of his movement, there
was no doubt to audiences that he was dancing. His inner lightness and
sensitivity was palpable. I imagine that Cunningham's diminishing ability to dance must have been a source of great personal frustration and
rage. But his desire to perform trumped the difficulties and led him to
find great expressiveness despite the limits on his ability to move.

Limits are a necessary partner in the creative act as well as in the
crafting of a successful life. What matters is the ability to look around
and accurately recognize what is working for you and what is working
against you, adjusting to the realities of the situation and mining the
potential of the limits with invention and energy.

Chapter 5

Opposition

The essence of art is form: it is to defeat oppositions, to conquer opposing forces, to create coherence from every centrifugal force, from all things that have been deeply and eternally alien to one another before and outside the form.

(Georg Lukács, philosopher)

When I was artistic director of Trinity Repertory Company in Providence, Rhode Island, I invited Molly Smith to direct a play as part of our 1989–90 season. Molly is an impressive, confident woman of action who founded the Perseverance Theater in Juneau, Alaska, and later became the highly successful artistic director of Arena Stage in Washington DC. At Trinity, she chose to stage a new adaptation of José Donoso's novel *Obscene Bird of Night*. During Molly's residency at Trinity I was struggling with the theater's board, company and community and the issues felt at times insurmountable. Molly, who grew up in Alaska and who is no stranger to the gigantic power of the natural world, advised me to *lean in*. Kayaking on a river and faced with an explosion of rough, dangerous water, one's natural inclination is to lean away from the turbulence and paddle for safety in the opposite direction. This, Molly said, is a big mistake. You must, on the contrary, lean into the apex of the turbulence, aim directly towards the problem. Only by joining the current's power can you eventually find your way to safety.

Of course Molly was not talking to me about kayaking, rather she was advising me about how I should negotiate the rough and dangerous currents that were swirling around me at the time at Trinity. In moments of great adversity, when one's body is screaming "run away!" retreat is not always the most effective action. The wisest move often feels counter-intuitive.

I took Molly's advice. I did lean in to the current. To this day I feel that the struggle was positive and that I stirred up issues that needed to be faced by Trinity's board, company and community. The engagement was worth it even though my tenure there only lasted for one year.

The artistic process often requires one to act in opposition to what feels natural. For example, one's natural impulse is to run away from danger because for thousands of years humans have run away in order to survive in the primitive world. And yet the creative act asks for trust and engagement rather than fear and flight. Other examples of acting in opposition to what feels natural: to find balance it is necessary to welcome imbalance; to create an impression of rising one must be rooted deep into the ground; moving fast externally requires a concomitant internal stillness, rather than forcing things to happen; a theater director leans in to who is present and what they are already doing. These are all acts of opposition to what feels natural, even compelling.

The highly politicized Chinese artist Ai Wei Wei says that he does not provoke conflict, rather that all of his work is a reaction to what is happening to him at the moment. But, he adds, although he does not initiate action, he does push back a little at what is coming at him. "And when you push back," he declares, "something always happens." Both T'ai Chi Ch'uan and Aikido, martial arts from China and Japan respectively, teach practitioners to engage in conflict not by resisting but rather by joining the force of the oncoming adversary. In the joining, a transformation ensues. In order to be effective while holding the reins at Trinity, I acted in opposition to my impulse to flee and instead I leaned in, joining the natural power of the oncoming force. But leaning in to the current did not mean overpowering it.

Impulse vs. intuition

In his Nobel acceptance speech in 2006, the Turkish writer Orhan Pamuk claimed that he does not write to tell a story but rather he writes to *compose* a story. The difference, I believe, is instructive. Stories, like improvisations, can initially flow out easily, unrestrained, in a burst of communication. But to *compose* a story requires restraint, enforced distance, passionate intimacy and editing.

To compose either oneself or a work of art, it is necessary to transcend base and ancient human impulses and inclinations, bypass the ancient flight-or-fight impulses and act from the most advanced parts of the human brain. The latest evolutionary addition, the frontal cortex, modulates emotions, postpones gratification and makes executive decisions and long-term planning possible. To compose requires conscious restraint followed by the guidance of intuition. Impulse is different from intuition. Impulses tend to be automatic, instinctive and self-protective.

Intuition, on the other hand, is a process that allows you to know something directly without analytic reasoning, bridging the conscious and unconscious parts of the mind as well as joining instinct and reason.

Perhaps I became a theater director in an attempt to temper, control and re-compose the onslaught of chaos that I felt coming at me from the turbulent surrounding world and my own inner landscape. I sensed that in order to be successful, I had to harness my general unfocused fear, anger and panic and transform them into the fuel for creating. It was only by applying restraint and patience that I could begin to work steadily and intuitively.

Compression vs. expression

When angry, irritated or confronted with a challenging obstacle, the natural human propensity is to vent one's feelings, to lose one's temper, to throw a tantrum or to turn in on oneself. The artist, on the other hand, hopefully learns to tame the energy of anger and aggravation, store it and then draw upon it when needed in the service of artistic expression. The rage that I accumulated in childhood and continuing on into adult life, triggered by frustrating circumstances, setbacks and myriad bad reviews in *The New York Times*, have also provided me the necessary fuel for productive action and artistic expressivity.

The key to expression is compression because expression is the *consequence* of compression. Actors, musicians, visual artists and writers learn to restrain, to gather together and to compress energy, before releasing it into articulate action. Expression is earned by compression. The gathering in, the compression, can fill the ensuing action with power and clarity, transforming inarticulate irritation and frustration into eloquent, communicative shape and form.

Balance vs. imbalance

A play begins when something goes wrong, when the pendulum swings too wildly and an individual or a family or a society is thrown into a compromised state of imbalance. The world of a play is off-kilter. The story is generally the dramatization of an off-kilter world being brought back to some kind of stability.

As an artist and as a person I know that I must cultivate a taste for imbalance because I understand that expression happens in the heroic attempt to find balance from a state of imbalance. Dance training teaches performers to welcome the state of imbalance and to use it creatively. Actors, in order to speak a monologue successfully, must jump off a figurative cliff and carve the event of speaking during the downward trajectory. Rather than stopping between words or in the midst of sentences, paragraphs or between the lines of a dialogue, actors must keep breathing and speaking and allow nuances and expression to arise in the act of speaking, in the midst of flight.

Biologically the body requires a balanced state and physical equilibrium to maintain life. For this reason it is natural for humans to gravitate towards stability and balance. And yet, despite this natural human tendency and in exact opposition to what feels natural, creation generally occurs from an imbalanced state.

An actor knows that a living room couch can be the enemy. A soft couch on stage predisposes the actor's body to sink, cutting off access to the abdomen, making speaking difficult and robbing breath and energy from the body. To solve this problem, the actor must consciously compromise his or her stability and sit in a way that demands intense effort and composure to maintain. And yet to the audience it should look natural and comfortable. The effort and difficulty of imbalance allows the actor to breathe properly and speak with a connection to their abdomen. The body fights to maintain verticality while what the audience sees is horizontality.

Public vs. private

Perhaps a definition of acting for the theater is being private in public. How does an actor maintain intimacy in public? Constantin Stanislavsky articulated the actor's paradox and dilemma succinctly: you are in a living room and you are about to confess love for the first time to the only other person in the room. The situation is deeply personal, private and exposed. *And* there are a thousand people watching.

To flourish in the space between the two opposing forces of public and private requires imagination, patience and an ability to allow an audience to share in one's private experience. Rather than extending outwards, towards the audience, the actor creates a strong inner presence that draws the audience towards him or her.

Up vs. down

In the morning I awaken loaded down with the weight of entropy and sleep. It is difficult to get out of bed and I would prefer to turn over, kiss my wife and go back to sleep. I long to delay the crisis of stepping out into the world. What gets me up? Perhaps the hope for a good day or a promise made the night before helps me to swing my legs over the side of the bed. Acts of engagement, including meeting each day with a positive attitude, require effort, will, desire and an emotionally charged image of how things might be.

As we age, we lose energy; we begin to fall apart, to disorganize. Our lives lead inevitably to decay and death. As defined by thermodynamics, entropy is an increase of disorganization and it is a part of daily life. Without diligence and effort we can easily sink into lethargy and collapse. I admire an elderly person who grooms and dresses smartly because I know that this action is an achievement of resistance and opposition to diminishing energy and the force of entropy.

An artist also works in opposition to the weight of daily life in order to find lightness and buoyancy in artistic expression. The immense strain and cost of making art should not be visible to an audience. It is good to enjoy the airy flight of a ballerina but do not look at her torn and swollen feet. The lower to the ground an actor's body, the more opposite, upward, vertical energy is required. Horizontality requires an opposing verticality. The acquired lightness is what makes an artistic encounter with dark matter bearable.

Director/playwright Bertolt Brecht said that an actor, while walking downstage, should be thinking about *not* walking upstage. The actor can consciously create the space behind her or him as they move downstage. This too is opposition.

Actors grouped closely together onstage tend to collapse into one another, both energetically and physically. Once again, it is necessary to act against the natural inclination with oppositional force. Similarly, actors have a habit of looking directly at one another incessantly in a scene, perhaps in an attempt to sustain a connection. In order to act in opposition to this default inclination, it is necessary to consciously select moments of direct eye contact. In this way, the direct contact has more meaning for the audience.

Fast vs. slow

Perhaps the artistic impulse is a struggle against death, an effort to affirm life in the face of the certainty of dying. In contrast to the entropic directionality of a life cycle, art works in opposition to a living organism's tendency towards slowing down, dissolution and finally death. The artist searches for quickness, lightness and exactitude in the face of rot and decay. Fueled by curiosity, energy and hope, the artist enters and accepts the darkness and in that acceptance sometimes discovers a thin vein of light.

As I discussed in the previous chapter, the choreographer Merce Cunningham continued to dance late into his eighties. Towards the end of his life, he danced onstage sitting in a chair. And yet he danced. Despite the minimalism of his movement, the audience experienced only a transcendent lightness and quickness. And those who knew Cunningham's work from his early days recognized the irony. In his younger years, the choreographer was known for a piece in which he danced with great abandon with a chair strapped onto his back. Now, sitting in his chair in performance, Cunningham continued to accelerate his energy against the gradual expiration of entropy. The audience experienced his personal and political act of dignity, his act of defiance and his act of life.

During the process of a lifetime, the human body begins to slow down and gradually disintegrates. Similarly, every action, even every gesture, tends to disintegrate towards its conclusion. This deceleration and disintegration, confirmed by the rules of physics, is natural. In the theater each gesture, each physical action, each sentence, each dramatic encounter, each scene and each act, left to nature, will decelerate toward its ending. Actors, playwrights, directors and designers work together to oppose this tendency with an acceleration of energy so that the end of each gesture, action, sentence, dialogue, scene or act possesses more energy than the beginning.

Gustav Mahler's symphonies generally conclude in long sustained quietness. But the quietness, if played correctly, is the most demanding part for a musician and must be filled with great intensity and vigor. Similarly, an actor requires maximum energy in the quietest moments. A stage whisper demands far more energy than a loud moment. It would be natural to assume that quiet moments required the least energy to perform and yet the truth is that to sustain quiet drawn-out moments demands a tremendous amount of energy.

Audiences also naturally get tired and their perceptual abilities lose steam over time. Knowing this, the artist must compensate for the audience's growing fatigue, accelerating their own energy over time, counterbalancing the diminishing energy of the audience.

On the other hand, when encountering tough moments the natural inclination is to speed up. But the artist moves in opposition to this proclivity and, in the midst of complexity and difficulty, consciously slows down. The challenge is to savor the distress of challenging obstacles and to move *slowly* through them.

Known vs. unknown

It is a natural human propensity to divide the world around us into narrow categories. From fear or terror of the unknown, we cement our opinions and definitions of people, objects and places quickly, and these assumptions hold a mighty power over our lives.

My own natural proclivity is to categorize the world around me, to remove unfamiliar objects from their dangerous perches by defining, compartmentalizing and labeling them. I want to know what things are and I want to know where they are and I want to control them. I want to remove the danger of the unknown and replace it with the known. I want to feel safe. I want to feel out of danger.

And yet, as an artist, I know that I must welcome the strange and the unintelligible into my awareness and into my working process. Despite my propensity to own and control everything around me, my job is to "make the familiar strange and the strange familiar," as Bertolt Brecht recommended: to un-define and un-tame what has been delineated by belief systems and conventions, and to welcome the discomfort of doubt and the unknown, aiming to make visible what has become invisible by habit.

Because life is filled with habit, because our natural desire is to make countless assumptions and treat our surroundings as familiar and unthreatening, we need art to wake us up. Art un-tames, reifies and wakes up the parts of our lives that have been put to sleep and calcified by habit. The artist, or indeed anyone who wants to turn daily life into an adventure, must allow people, objects and places to be dangerous and freed from the definitions that they have accumulated over time.

Artifice vs. "the thing that cannot be faked"

No matter how tragic the role, actors strive for the impression of lightness, ease, naturalness and a sense of evanescent effortlessness. And yet, it is impossible to engender this lightness, this sensation of naturalness, by going directly for it. Imagine saying to someone standing onstage in front of an audience, "Act naturally! Speak naturally!" The lightness, the necessary quickness, spontaneity, agility and ability to leap from thought to thought, line to line, demands rigor and training transcending anything that happens easily or naturally.

The great vaudeville comedian W. C. Fields notoriously said, "Never work with animals or children." Animals and children, due to their lack of artifice and self-consciousness, are often cute, almost always interesting and draw the audience's attention without fail. They steal focus because their actions are not artificial or fake and their unpredictability makes them interesting to watch. And yet, successful theater balances two opposite conditions: the artificial and "the thing that cannot be faked."

Pablo Picasso said, "It took me four years to paint like Raphael, but a lifetime to paint like a child." An artist walks a tight rope between artifice and the untamed. Technique, which is part of the realm of artifice, is necessary in order to arrive at the desired state of naturalness. The artist must go through the back door in order to arrive at the front. To walk naturally upon the stage, the actor must rediscover the awkwardness of walking for the very first time. Similarly, the act of speaking requires reinvention.

Here are a few examples of "the thing that cannot be faked": an actor notices a beeper going off in the back of a theater; real water, earth, air or fire; real physical effort; tangible kinesthetic response between actors and between the audience and the actors; the physical effect of live voices on the bodies of the audience.

Examples of artifice: crafted visual metaphor; a red scarf that stands in for blood; the number of steps that the actor counts to back up to a wall; the angle of a hand in a shaft of light; the notated music of a song; memorized words.

In the theater, the balancing act between the artificial and "the thing that cannot be faked" is an ongoing challenge. A production with too much of "the thing that cannot be faked" and not enough artifice suffers by feeling chaotic, blurry and unclear to the audience. Too much artifice and too little of "the thing that cannot be faked," the experience will feel studied, synthetic and cold.

The glorious energy of the untamed and uncontrollable requires the counterpoint artifice of choice, craft and repetition. The audience's experience is made all the richer by the play between the controlled and the uncontrolled, the restrained and the unrestrained, the artifice and the real. But the balance must be right.

Phenomenology vs. structuralism vs. semiotics

In 1976 and 1977 I was fortunate to attend the graduate program in Drama at NYU, now known as Performance Studies. The program encouraged students to study performance through the lenses of anthropology, sociology and non-theatrical critical systems. Learning to think this way had an enormous impact on the way I approach the theater to this day. I learned that there are no right or wrong methods of criticism, but rather radically different ways to look at the same event.

I learned to examine performance from three fundamentally different perspectives: phenomenology, structuralism and semiotics. Each of these modes of analysis allowed me to consider the same performance from three completely different points of view, each offering contrasting ways to appreciate and analyze the experience.

Phenomenology focuses on the structural subjective experience of consciousness. Most mainstream theater criticism is phenomenological, emphasizing the visceral experience of a performance with primacy on how the body perceives it, how the experience *hits* the perceiver. "I loved it," "I hated it," "It sent shivers up my spine," "The actress has such a beautiful body." These statements and impressions are phenomenological. Phenomenology is not concerned with concepts, metaphors or abstract thinking; rather, it is the world of appearances and affect.

Structuralism, first articulated by Claude Lévi-Strauss in the 1950s, proposes that a work of art can be understood objectively by means of its structure. The attention in structuralism is not given to ideas or human imagination. Structuralism is less interested in interpreting what a work means than in explaining how it can insinuate what it means by showing its implicit rules and conventions. The emphasis of structuralism is on the logic and mechanics of how a work is constructed.

Finally, semiotics concerns itself exclusively with the creation of meaning. Semiotics examines how signs, symbols, icons, analogies and metaphors combine to generate meaning. Semiotics draws attention to the layers of meaning that may be embodied in simple representations. Memory and imagination are joined in the creation of meaning.

Learning about phenomenology, structuralism and semiotic ways of perceiving taught me that there is no right or wrong way to receive information; rather, I can consciously choose the lens through which I want to experience the event.

Onstage vs. offstage

An artist is like a notorious criminal in pursuit by a detective. The detective is the audience. If the artist/criminal leaves too many clues behind, the audience/detective will lose interest in the chase. If two few clues are left behind, the audience/detective will get distracted and also lose interest. A balance between the known and the unknown must be struck and renewed constantly. An artist makes conscious decisions about what to show and what to keep hidden in order to keep up the suspense of co-creation with an audience.

The ancient Greeks taught through example that it is best to leave the most violent actions offstage. Clytemnestra leads Agamemnon and Cassandra offstage to their bloody deaths. Agave rips her son to pieces offstage. There is no way to embody an equivalent of what the audience can so powerfully imagine. The audience reconstructs the full horror of these events through a messenger's words and their own subjective imagery.

The etymology of the word "obscene" may ultimately be traced to the Greek *ob-skene*, literally "offstage." For an artist, the key is to figure out what to show and what to leave to the audience's imagination. Great horror movies leave the most potent imagery to the audience's imagination. The grade B movies that show all the gore end up simply looking silly. Alfred Hitchcock displayed his brilliance in the film *Psycho* by carefully choosing what *not* to show in the famous shower/murder scene.

Human beings are expectation machines, physiologically and neurologically designed to anticipate what will happen next. This human trait, which almost certainly originated in ancient survival tactics, makes time-based performance a potential minefield of fulfilled and broken expectations. In music a melody is the composer's way of setting up an expectation. What happens to that melody? Does it return? Does it return as the same or different? The artist is faced consistently with one choice: to fulfill or to break the expectation. Both options can be dramatic.

Alfred Hitchcock, in an interview with French director François Truffaut, explained that if a character appears from screen-left, the audience generally trusts and likes the person because most western cultures read from left to right and an entrance from the left creates a sense of familiarity and friendliness. If a character arrives from screen-right the audience generally suspects that he or she is sinister or dangerous. In Hitchcock's film *Rebecca*, the forbidding Mrs. Danvers always appears from screen-right, unexpectedly and then motionless. Subliminally, the audience expects something bad to happen.

Every moment of a play, as in every measure of a piece of music, sets up expectations about what will follow. The syncopations of expectations, consciously fulfilled and broken, can make for a compelling journey for the audience. A plot point that is too easily predicted is also too easily forgotten. An image, an action or an object not immediately recognizable arouses concern, curiosity and vigilance on the part of the viewer and therefore tends to become inexplicably vivid in her or his imagination.

Old vs. new

Each time that I direct a classic play or opera, I fill myself up with as much information as I can find about its production history. I read theoretical writing about the play, and study the context in which the play originally occurred. I fill myself up with the old in order to find something new.

We make new things upon the skeletons of the old. The more we can incorporate the old bones into the work, the more tensile strength will hold it up. In making his film *Raging Bull*, director Martin Scorsese had trouble figuring out how to edit the final fight scene between the boxers Jake LaMotta and Sugar Ray Robinson. He ended up using Alfred Hitchcock's original shot list from the shower sequence in *Psycho* as his template. The jarring editing technique in both films portrays the protagonists' subjective experience of violence.

For me, one of the richest sources of inspiration for the theater can be found in Russian film director Sergei Eisenstein's theories about montage and editing. In the early part of the twentieth century he used his understanding of language to invent a system of composition by linking separate ideas together, juxtaposing them and creating new meanings through syntactical choices in arrangement.

Survival vs. gift

The artistic impulse operates in opposition to the Darwinian drive towards the survival of the fittest; it originates in the impulse to give a gift to another person. Art is not innately a transaction nor is it competitive. It does not directly put food on the table or lead to sexual congress or abiding power. Making art is a liminal ambiguous activity and makes no logical sense. We are not making art for the money and when money becomes a dominating factor, the art loses its magnificence, its munificence and its inherent wonder.

The artistic process requires us to learn how to flourish in the paradoxical realm of opposition, in the space between conflicting ideas, in the opposing dynamics within our own bodies, in expectations fulfilled and broken, in the act of leaning in towards oncoming turbulence, in the necessity for restraint when all riled up, in the requirement to cultivate intimacy in public, to accelerate energy and speed in light of the human tendency towards entropy and decay, between what we know and what we can never know, between technique and what comes naturally, among the various ways to see the same event, between what is visible and what is invisible and between what is new and what came before.

Chapter 6

Arrest

Nothing is a mistake.

(Merce Cunningham, choreographer)

I do not remember now what brought me to a local movie theater in Montreal in 1978 to see *Sommergäste*, a film from West Berlin. But I do remember the feeling of arrest afterwards. I sat stunned and speechless from the impact of what I had just experienced. I struggled to read the screen credits for any clues about the creators. Because the credits were in German, which I did not speak, I could only make out that the film was directed by Peter Stein based upon Maxim Gorky's play *Summerfolk*, in collaboration with a company called the Schaubühne.

Even though *Sommergäste* was a film, it had all the hallmarks of theater. I found out soon afterwards that the Schaubühne was indeed a critically acclaimed and politically driven theater company based in West Berlin. But I had never encountered theater like it, at once aesthetically stunning, emotionally rich, politically awake and beautifully acted. In the American theater I was accustomed to productions with gorgeous stage pictures but lacking in emotion or complex ideas. I had seen works of great intelligence but deficient in humor or beauty. I had experienced politically oriented work, but the didacticism ultimately did not touch my heart. In *Sommergäste* everything seemed to be happening simultaneously: aesthetics, humor, emotionality, politics and intelligence.

Stopped in my tracks by the experience of *Sommergäste*, I was at a loss about what to do. I knew in my bones that I had to do something, *anything*. I needed to act; I needed to move *towards* the utopian vision of theater that I had glimpsed so briefly. The very next morning, lacking any other ideas about how to proceed, I signed up for German language classes at the local Goethe Institute in Montreal. I was now following a red thread.

At the Goethe Institute I discovered the glossy German monthly magazine *Theater Heute* (*Theater Today*). Because the Schaubühne was quite popular in Germany at the time, each issue of *Theater Heute* featured their newest production. I studied each and every detail of the sleek photographs and begged anyone who spoke German to translate the in-depth articles that accompanied the photos. The ideas in the magazines introduced me to new ways of thinking about theater, about acting, about the possible juxtapositions between political and social ideas, about visual design and about philosophical notions of the theater's place in society. And then I began to use what I found there in my own work.

The Schaubühne am Halleschen Ufer, later the Schaubühne am Lehniner Platz, was founded in 1962 as a private theater that specialized in politically and socially conscious productions. The Peter Stein years, 1970–85, propelled the Schaubühne into world consciousness, and eventually into my own consciousness, by bringing political fire and high aesthetics together. A talented team of young theater-makers joined the director Stein at the Schaubühne and their aim was to present nothing short of an alternative to the standard German state theater by means of new, cooperative forms. First and foremost, the theater, unlike all of the large state and city theaters of Germany, Austria and Switzerland, purported to be a democracy. Everyone involved in the institution – actors, dramaturgs, administration and technical staff – was supposed to have equal say. The collective effort and the productions reflected, as closely as possible within the context of a director's theater, joint ownership of the dramaturgical process.

All of this was new to me.

I eventually returned to New York City from Montreal, and continued studying German. I begged for details whenever I met anyone who had seen a production at the Schaubühne first-hand. I am not moderate in my addictions. I soaked in every word, digested the ideas and began to incorporate the concepts into my own productions. I memorized the date and year of each Schaubühne production, the name of every actor, and made a close study of Peter Stein and the other directors who worked with the Schaubühne acting company, including Klaus Michael Gruber and Luc Bondy. I applied their radical new ideas about collaboration, politics and acting to my street, rough, low/no budget work in the downtown scene in New York City.

Inevitably my friends, who by now knew about my obsession with all things German, encouraged German-speaking theater people visiting New York to call me on the telephone. "Talk to Anne," they would say, "she loves German theater." Soon I was receiving phone calls from people with thick German accents, "Hello, my name is Georg and I am in New York to learn about experimental theater and American spontaneity." I invited these curious Germans to my rehearsals and afterwards interrogated them: "Have you seen anything at the Schaubühne?" If they answered "yes," I invited them to a café to interrogate them late into the night for details of all things Schaubühne. My hunger felt insatiable.

Eventually I met the actress Sabine Andreas, a longtime member of the Schaubühne who was visiting New York after leaving the company. I remembered her vividly from *Sommergäste*. Over the course of several months, I was able to ask her detailed and in-depth questions about Peter Stein's rehearsal methods. She showed great enthusiasm for my own work and seemed delighted to talk about her years with the Schaubühne. I translated all of this new influence into my rehearsals and continued to study German. Finally I was able to read *Theater Heute* without assistance.

Occasionally I cast German-speaking actors in my shows and eventually many German, Swiss and Austrian audiences came to see my rough and ready site-specific productions in New York City. Two years after seeing *Sommergäste* in Montreal, two years after my obsession with the Schaubühne began, two years after I began to appropriate the contents of the pages of *Theater Heute*, a six-page article about my own work came out in *Theater Heute*. "This is the new American theater," the magazine announced. The irony did not escape me.

Due to the article in *Theater Heute*, I received numerous invitations to direct in Germany, Austria and Switzerland. I accepted every one. The invitations provided, in my way of thinking, the opportunity to escape what I saw then as the superficiality of the American theater scene. I vowed not to speak English. I wanted to become like the Germans and make theater like the Germans. I left the United States with little regret and began a journey that, in the end, brought me back home again to New York with unexpected insights and new perspectives that I never could have imagined beforehand. I returned home with a new mission. But the journey was rough and included massive doses of failure.

Initially hired to direct graduating actors from the acting academy in West Berlin in 1981, I proposed a collaboratively created piece that would capture the current zeitgeist of West Berlin. The creative process lasted five months, finally culminating in performances of *Leb oder Tot* (*Live or Dead*), a devised play about the house-squatting scene in Berlin, a very hot topic in those days. But ultimately the prolonged exploratory and development process proved far more interesting than the play that we created together. The performances were disastrous.

During the process of rehearsal, I contracted a disease (dis-ease) that most Germans know intimately. The condition is known as *angst*. Angst is gray, lives in the gut and paralyzes the soul. Perhaps the Germans are particularly familiar with angst because of their complex, violent history. Full of angst, I gained weight and drank a great deal of alcohol. My stuck-ness, visible in my body, permeated into the rehearsal hall. I eventually lost every ounce of spontaneity, play, ease and even joy. I finally understood why so many Germans came to New York City to learn about American spontaneity. I found very little spontaneity in the German theater.

While Americans excel in spontaneity, the Germans are fanatical about rigor and *genauigkeit* (exactitude) and spend exorbitant amounts of time in concentrated text analysis. Intent upon working like the German theater artists and fearful of being seen as a superficial American, I consciously abandoned my downtown postmodern roots. I mistrusted my instincts, was terrified of working choreographically and worried about making choices arbitrarily. And so we paddled on for the many months of rehearsal and development for *Leb oder Tot*. Profoundly lost, I was unable to bring any rigor, passion, shape or exactitude to the process. I was simply anxious. The final product was vague and expensive, unformed and not rooted in any personal necessity.

Each night the theater filled to capacity, but audiences hated the show. "Dieses ist Scheiße" (this is shit) they shouted and occasionally threw fruit at the stage. Ultimately I agreed with them. The work embarrassed me intensely. Like the production, I felt unmasked, unconnected and half-baked.

One morning, towards the end of *Leb oder Tot* and near the conclusion of my time in Berlin, I was having breakfast in a bar (on the weekends, Germans often eat breakfast in bars) and a young man in a brown leather jacket approached me aggressively. "You directed that play at the HdK, right?" he asked. "Yes," I answered. He launched into a litany of everything that he hated about the production. My will to live crumpled at this final indignity. I left the bar abruptly, headed home, packed my suitcases and left on a train bound for Italy. I needed a break. I needed to collapse. I needed to get away.

In Italy I got off the train in the northern alpine town of Bolzano, closed myself into a room in a local *pensione* and essentially fell apart. At the end of a week I emerged from the room but something in me had shifted. From the depths of my despair and frustration, I realized that I was, in fact, American. My sense of humor, my instincts, my feeling for structure is all American. I realized with relief that I did not need to be embarrassed by my own culture. The shoulders upon which I stand are generous and wide. The United States has a rich complex history, full of paradox, contradictions and conflict. For political reasons our cultural history is constantly on the verge of being forgotten, misremembered and swept under the next available rug. Gore Vidal called us the *United States of Amnesia*. I arrived at a new mission: to study, to absorb and to remember (re-member) our cultural history. With this realization, I continued on to Bern, Switzerland for my next job. If I could manage to direct another play after the failure in Berlin, then I might really be a director, I thought.

Arriving in the city of Bern in the midst of the Swiss Alps, I was ready to work. From the first rehearsals, I felt a new personal freedom and a connection to my North American roots. I was able to be spontaneous and joyful and to commit to the violent act of decisiveness based largely upon trust in my own intuition.

I learned a great deal from the failure and the pain of my Berlin experience. In my attempt to imitate the Germans, I discovered that I am profoundly American. Like the conclusions of most fairy tales, I returned home to my own back yard to unearth the riches that I had been searching for. Since then much of my work in the theater investigates what it means to be American.

This circular and yet critical journey and adventure, so crucial to my growth as an artist, was ultimately instigated by the state of arrest brought about by a German film by Peter Stein and the Schaubühne. Stopped in my tracks, I changed direction and the world opened up for me in ways that I never could have imagined or predicted. In retrospect I see that the state of arrest provoked by *Sommergäste* was actually an important crossroads in my life's trajectory. And I see now that there have been many crossroads along the way that always seem to arrive when I least expect it. In the midst of an encounter like *Sommergäste*, I find myself both incapable of speech and unable to progress further along my life's prescribed trajectory. Standing at the crossroads, stopped by the force of an encounter with something new and exciting, I know in my bones that I must change my thinking and change my life's direction.

The first of these crossroads appeared when I was 15 years old in a theater in Providence, Rhode Island, during a production of Shakespeare's *Macbeth* at Trinity Repertory Company. Nothing in my life up until then had prepared me for this and the experience turned me into a theater director. I felt awe and longing for the magnitude, beauty and physical power that seemed just within reach. When the play was over, I sat stunned and at a complete loss for words. But within this physical state of arrest, I could sense the tiniest motion. My soul pointed towards the stage and wanted everything that I had just seen there. I wanted to be part of it; I wanted to make such things.

I have since learned that these moments of arrest, during which alternate universes are suddenly and unexpectedly visible, are the guidelines for my life as an artist. I must pay attention to the physical excitement and the emotional impact and then move in a new direction.

> Hope is what makes us strong. It is why we are here. It is what we fight with when all else is lost.
>
> (Pandora's last words)

In Greek mythology, Pandora was the first woman on earth. Created by Zeus, she was, as the etymology of her name indicates, well endowed. Aphrodite bestowed beauty upon her, Hermes gave her persuasiveness and the power of speech and Apollo gave her music. The beautiful Pandora evoked strong desire in all who saw her. In retribution for Prometheus's theft of fire, an angry Zeus gave Pandora a box, which she was told never to open, and then bequeathed her to Epimetheus, brother of Prometheus. But the gods and goddesses had also made Pandora curious and eventually she did open the box, out of which sprang disease, death and sorrow. Pandora realized what she had done, but could not slam the lid back fast enough. The only thing remaining in the jar was *Elpis*, or Hope.

Odysseus took ten long years to journey from Troy to Ithaca, during which time he was exposed to the awful and wonderful panoply of Pandora's box. We each, as Joseph Campbell wrote in his seminal *Hero with a Thousand Faces*, must make forays out into the unknown, journeys across our metaphorical Aegean Sea. Occasionally we have to look into Pandora's box and be shaken by what we see, shaken and stirred (emotionally) in order to move forward with the humble memory of what we have seen on the dark side.

An artist's occasional exposure to the contents of Pandora's box enriches and deepens his or her creative endeavor. But in choosing consciously to gaze into Pandora's box, it is important to know that the sight is not safe from any distance. To look inside is to be instantly infected and affected, and the reaction is guaranteed to be emotional and visceral. On the other hand, to avoid contact with the box for too long is risky for a working artist. If an artist shies away from exposure to the contents of Pandora's box for too long, her or his work will lack a certain force of reality that only exposure will endow.

I am interested in the latent potential within the silence that follows the arrest of a powerful or novel experience. When I am stopped by a fresh assault upon my senses, I am also wildly alive and the repercussions can be physical, psychic and transformative. In this gap, this arrest, this shakeup, this silence, a seed is planted.

As time went on I was able to identify these moments of physical immobility and speechlessness, these glances into Pandora's box, as fruitful places. What rendered me silent also eventually made me want to speak, to express, to communicate and to take action. I learned to identify my fear of change and began to welcome the necessity for an occasional, if not regular, encounter with what the French psychoanalyst/philosopher Jacques Lacan called "the Real."

> The Real is what resists symbolization absolutely.
>
> (Jacques Lacan, psychoanalyst)

Lacan proposed that humans interpret their experience of the world in three possible ways: the Imaginary, the Symbolic and the Real.

In a search for coherence, a child develops the capacity to form images or icons and also to identify with them. This Imaginary realm, developed in childhood, is part of the narcissistic formation of the ego in what Lacan called the "mirror" stage of wholeness and coherence, the internalized image of an ideal self. Examples of the Imaginary are: a fusion of child and parent, the idealization of older siblings, the eventual choice to emulate role models and heroes, imaginary friends. All are imagistic fantasies.

The Symbolic kingdom is made possible by culture, language and narrative and is supercharged by personal desire. By means of the Symbolic realm, I can place the situation in which I find myself into a context, which in turn dictates how I act. For example, in a classroom, the essential nature of the teacher–student relationship is Symbolic. I am the student and he is the teacher. Or I am the teacher and she is the student. Or I am the driver and she is the policewoman. I translate the world around me into a symbolic order and symbolic moments.

In contrast to the Imaginary and the Symbolic, the Real, because it resists representation, can feel frightening and incomprehensible. Words fail. The Real is unnamable, unknowable and lives outside of language, out of reach and out of our consciousness. It puts us into a state of arrest. The death of a close friend or relative, falling in love, the collapse of the World Trade Center towers or a powerful art experience are the kinds of events that can plunge us into seeing the world through the lens of the Real. The Real returns to arrest us in the moments when the Symbolic and the Imaginary begin to crack.

All art, to some extent, attempts to stand against the transient
nature of human experience by supplying an alternative vitality.

(Simon Schama, historian)

Perhaps when I have been separated for too long from exposure to the
Real, my life and work suffers in its absence. When the Symbolic and
the Imaginary dominate my day-to-day experience and I do not allow
for exposure to the Real, I live a lie. But despite my separation from it,
the Real continues to exert its influence in my life and my artistic
output. Possibly it is manifest in the sensation of dread or else a vague
sense of loss or hope that overwhelms me when least expected. I am not
immune and exposure to the Real can be either painful and disorienting
or galvanizing and inspirational. Generally, my assumptions and beliefs
are challenged by what I encounter there.

According to Lacan, we translate the Real into either the Imaginary
or the Symbolic in order to gain control over its profound nature.
Through the Imaginary, we transform the unfathomable, uncontainable
Real into palpable meaning through the invigorating power of imagery.
Essentially representational, the Imaginary objectifies and familiarizes
the Real by framing it in images and pictures. Similarly, in translating
the world into the Symbolic, we project meaning onto objects. A car,
for example, is more than a car; it is a symbol. A car can be a status
symbol as well as a functional method of travel. It is not only functional
but also psychological.

In a small crowded theater within an enormous Cineplex in southern
California in 1986, I saw Oliver Stone's meditation on the war in
Vietnam, *Platoon*. Emotionally and physically affected by the film, it took
a while after the final credits to pull myself together, to stand up to exit
the theater. Walking out I noticed that one of the theater seats was
covered in a shiny black plastic garbage bag. At that moment I imagined
that all around the country each and every cinema had chosen one seat to
wrap in black plastic as a metaphor for a fallen soldier who might have
been sitting there if not for the Vietnam War. I burst into tears. It did
not occur to me until much later that the seat was probably broken and
the Cineplex staff had placed a bag over it to prevent audience members
from sitting on a faulty seat. The experience of the film led me to bring
special meaning to the object. Through the filter of my experience, the
plastic bag transported me through the Symbolic and then on to the Real.

But the whole point about the Real is that the impossibility is not
the result of some positive obstacle, but is purely inherent: the
impossibility is produced as the very condition of symbolic space.

That is the ultimate paradox of the Real. You cannot have it all, not because there is something opposing you, but because of this purely formal, structurally inherent, self-blockade.

(Slavoj Žižek, philosopher)

The underlying existence of the Real is what gives the most persuasive art its power. The multiple layers of meanings that lurk and move inward towards the core are what give presence to a work of art. On the surface a story is told. A story is an access point for the reader, listener or spectator, and helps to keep him or her present and cognitively engaged. Then a great work begins to open out and resonate. The alchemy, the deep-rooted experience of a work of art, takes over. Rothko's paintings, which appear at first simply as fields of color, with time and experience expand and propel the viewer ever deeper into the painting. At the heart of a great artwork, the perceiver arrives in the proximity of its *secret cause*, an expression that James Joyce coined in *A Portrait of the Artist as a Young Man*. Science has its dark matter, visual art has its negative space. In the theater it is what is not obvious or immediately visible that is most important. What lies beneath is the issue. The Real is the presence of the unnamed, the *secret cause*.

To illustrate James Joyce's notion of the *secret cause*, I turn to a lucid example offered by mythologist Joseph Campbell, who, during a lecture, proposed a thought experiment: Imagine that a Mr. A shoots and kills a Mr. B. What, he asks, is the cause of Mr. B's death? What is the *secret cause* that lies at the heart of the action? Is it the bullet? According to Campbell, the bullet is the instrumental cause of Mr. B's death, but it is not the *secret cause*. The instrumental cause does not touch upon the tragic, which is what Joyce was after with the *secret cause*. Moving to the next level, Campbell proposes that Mr. A is a white man and Mr. B is a black man. Mr. A shoots and kills Mr. B. What is the cause? Is the cause of Mr. B's death racism? The reflection on racism, while instructive, has nothing tragic about it. Campbell goes on to admit that he chose the issue of black and white with the idea of Dr. Martin Luther King, Jr. A week or so before he walked to his death, King said, "I know that I am challenging death." His statement begins to approach the complexity and paradoxical nature of the *secret cause*, and the fact that he did not know that he was going to die makes it all the more poignant. Dr. Martin Luther King, in the performance of what became his destiny, consciously chose to threaten the limits. The *secret cause* exists in the fact that he was a man who brought his own limits into play. King was a heroic man and his story is tragic, a tragedy, in the very best sense of the word. As Aristotle said, the hero of the tragedy has both nobility and a certain fault. And the fault of Martin Luther King was the fact that he disrespected his limit. He headed directly at it.

> A photograph is a secret about a secret; the more it tells you, the less you know.
>
> (Diane Arbus, photographer)

We protect ourselves from the overwhelming chaos of the world through the convictions that we hold on to, the stories that we tell ourselves and the ethics and morals that we cultivate. These restraints are necessary and helpful in moving efficiently from one day to the next. But occasionally, say, when things start to fall apart, we are allowed a glimpse into the inferno of Pandora's box that reveals the true nature of the infinitely complex and paradoxical universe that we actually inhabit. The sight is usually overwhelming and precipitates physical, emotional and intellectual arrest. Normally we protect ourselves from such chaos. But an artist, for the sake of the art, has to be open to it.

At the age of 37 I was diagnosed with breast cancer and the lid of Pandora's box swung open once again in my direction. I saw with great urgency that time is not infinite; time is, rather, precious, and I cannot know when my life will come to an end. I made significant changes. I left a fully tenured professorship in San Diego and moved back east towards what I really wanted and dreamed of doing. I learned by looking into Pandora's box, by exposure to the Real, about the transitory nature of every instant. To this day, I do not choose a project that does not thrill and challenge me. Even though my medical prognosis is good, I retain a permanently altered attitude regarding time.

> The instant wherein that supreme quality of beauty, the clear radiance of the esthetic image, is apprehended luminously by the mind which has been arrested by its wholeness and fascinated by its harmony is the luminous silent stasis of esthetic pleasure, a spiritual state very like to that cardiac condition which the Italian physiologist, Luigi Galvani, using a phrase almost as beautiful as Shelley's, called the enchantment of the heart.
>
> (James Joyce, novelist)

I have experienced arrest many times in museums and art galleries. I am stopped by the paintings of Francis Bacon, the Scottish painter Peter Doig, the Americans Richard Diebenkorn and George Tooker and the Spanish sculptor Juan Muñoz. Once I am arrested, their works present me with nothing less than a sip of the eternal.

I have noticed a trend running rampant in museums: visitors snapping photos of the art on their cell phones. The phone seems to act as a medium between the observer and the observed, cutting off direct experience, authentic encounter and any chance of arrest. The phone captures the work of art and takes it hostage. Perhaps the phenomenon of cell phone photos speaks to a certain lackadaisical attitude towards both making and "consuming" art. Perhaps capturing art on a cell phone protects one from the danger of the Real, which lurks inside each enduring work.

The phenomenon of cell phone photos in museums seems to be related inextricably to consumer attitudes found in the theater, on both sides of the footlights. In the theater, high box office prices contribute to the audience's sense of ownership and entitlement and lead to a subservient and passive aggressive attitude on the part of the artists. The audience buys a product. If the product does not meet their approval or expectations, the consumers feel righteous about noisily and conspicuously exiting a performance. After all, they have bought the right to do as they please. Theater artists believe that they are serving up merchandise rather than sharing a process, and their objective becomes to please rather than to communicate.

What disturbs me on both counts, in theaters and in museums, is the consumer attitude adapted to the experience of art. In the theater, the attitude of righteous ownership deprives the audience of an encounter with the unfamiliar. In the museum, taking cell phone photographs distances the viewer from any potentially dangerous direct communion with the work of art itself. Perhaps the impulse to take photos is an attempt by the viewers not only to distance themselves from any possible danger of aesthetic arrest, but it also allows them to store the experience and contend with it in a time, place and condition of their choosing.

The playwright Alan Bennett wrote in his diary after seeing a Vermeer exhibit in Delft: " I have a sense of vertigo, though, in the presence of great paintings, as when standing on a cliff and feeling oneself pulled to the edge." I do not imagine that Alan Bennett arrived at the exhibit equipped with a cell phone camera. Why take a cell phone photo of a work of art except to make the object smaller, more controllable and less threatening?

We live in a world that increasingly insulates us from powerful encounters with art. Conductor Daniel Barenboim in his book entitled *Music Quickens Time* suggests that hearing ubiquitous music in bookstores, shopping malls and at the dentist replaces the participation of the intellect in listening to music with passive consumption. What's missing is the potential for transformation that actively listening to music can provoke. Barenboim describes the act of listening as "hearing with thought." He takes the notion further. Feeling is memory with thought. Memory comes easily, immediately and directly to us, whereas recollection can only come through reflection and individual effort.

In the theater, each time that we approach a play or a role we also choose an attitude. If our intention is to dominate, control or be superior, we tend to make the play or the role smaller than we are. When an actor says, "my character would not do that," I know that she or he has made the character smaller. How do we enter the arena of a rehearsal or performance? Is it possible to allow the play, our colleagues and the audience to be dangerous and unknowable in a way that will render us more courageous and also more respectful?

The late great actress and teacher Stella Adler insisted that all her acting students arrive in class properly attired, coats and ties for men and dresses for women. No jeans, no shorts. She insisted that they approach the arena of acting with respect and civility. According to actor Jason Grant, who studied with her, Adler herself "made her entrance wearing a blue knit dress, high heels, a mink coat draped over her shoulders. She sat down, the coat fell away onto the chair, and then class began." Adler insisted that everyone in the room approach one another with care, bringing their best foot forward, allowing for unexpected encounters.

> Let's assume that we have a set number of days to indent the world with our beliefs, to find and create the beauty that only a finite existence allows for, to wrestle with the question of purpose and wrestle with our answers.
>
> (Jonathan Safran Foer, novelist)

Our creative forces are cunning in constructing a palpable life in which we do not need, too often, to stare into the dark matter, the Pandora's box that lies in wait and is always available to us. But time and again critical events bring us into contact with the yawning jaws of Pandora's box. In the crisis of the breakup of a love relationship we are brought face to face with the reality that one is born alone, lives alone and is bound by the experience of the body's perimeters. And that perhaps we have failed. Perhaps we miss someone terribly. A crisis of faith, when the religion that we had leaned upon is brought into question, and in its place lives an enormous disappointment or despair. Upon the death of a loved one, one is confronted with the absolute fact of mortality. Some of the greatest works of art were animated by grief or pain or an attempt to find order and harmony in what is in actuality a disharmonious universe: William Styron's *Darkness Visible*, Vincent Van Gogh's *Starry Night*, Virginia Woolf's *Between the Acts*, Gustav Mahler's *Kindertotenlieder* and Sylvia Plath's *Daddy*.

And yet it is not necessary to be depressed, suicidal or willing to die for a vision of the future to create art that is informed by occasional encounters with the contents of Pandora's box, with the Real. The myth of Pandora is instructive in its emphasis on hope. Great art is exuberant and emanates a contagious sense of excitement. The exposure to Pandora's box can be life-giving and transformative.

Chapter 7

Spaciousness

The stream and the broken pottery: what was any art but an effort to make a sheath, a mould in which to imprison for a moment the shining, elusive element which is life itself – life hurrying past us and running away, too strong to stop, too sweet to lose?

(Willa Cather, novelist)

As a teenager, the experience of reading Virginia Woolf's novel *To the Lighthouse* became a landmark in my development as an artist. Initially I found the book difficult, requiring effort and perseverance. Then a little more than halfway through, something unexpected happened. There I was, sweating through the complex, tangled, unfamiliar narrative and suddenly I felt a trap door open and ... I fell through. I remember the sense of free fall. Spaciousness. Freedom. The book had led to a release and a sensation of timelessness. And this free-fall experience of spaciousness is what I strive to recreate in my work for audiences in the theater.

Each and every moment of existence, no matter how stressful or how fleeting, contains the potential for spaciousness. The word spaciousness normally implies place but it can also encompass qualities of time, of relationships and of presence. A popular yogic Sanskrit chant, *Lokah Samasta Sukhino Bhavantu*, is normally translated, "May all beings everywhere be happy and free from suffering." The word *Sukhino* refers to happiness, joy or freedom. But the word can also be translated as spaciousness. I find the kinship between happiness and spaciousness useful.

Chronos vs. kairos

The ancient Greeks conceived of time in two radically different ways and produced two different words to distinguish one from the other:

chronos and *kairos*. In English, we have to make do with only one word: *time*. This "making do" has led to confusion about these two fundamentally different means of experiencing time. *Chronos* is measured time. *Kairos* is unbound and unmeasured time. *Chronos* is quantitative while *kairos* is qualitative. *Chronos* is chronological time. The difference between *chronos* and *kairos* is the difference between time and timing. Any moment can be experienced as either one or the other.

Neither *chronos* nor *kairos* is time itself. *Chronos* is a particular way of understanding time by the clock. *Chronos* is chronology. It is measurement. *Kairos*, on the other hand, is timing or opportunity. Our current cultural moment of digital frenzy has obliged us as a culture to be super attentive to *chronos*. Our lives are generally segmented into time sequences and deadlines and schedules and calendars and hourly to-dos. We wear watches, which we refer to perhaps too often. More often than not other people's opinions of us are based upon our success with time-management.

My upbringing instilled in me a proclivity towards *chronos*. Growing up in a Navy family I was taught to be hyperconscious of chronological time. I was expected to be on time, without fail, and if not on time, to arrive early. Family outings were awkward. At picnics, invited events and excursions, we would be the first family to arrive and then, of course, we were the first to leave. It seemed to me that we left before the fun even got started. Even today *chronos* is my default setting. I measure time incessantly. I am generally uptight and nervous about punctuality. I am hyperaware of time and I check it constantly. I wake up as if I have an alarm clock implanted in my brain. Just before leaving home for work I panic about being late. I arrive everywhere early. In some ways I am proud of my punctuality and expect it from others. But I also recognize my predisposition to be a prisoner of *chronos*.

Without vigilance, I feel that I am too easily sucked into the experience of time as *chronos*, regular time, one minute at a time, staring down the clock until the work day is over time, 30 excruciating minutes in traffic time, "when are we going to get there?" time and two hours till lunch time. *Chronos* is the hard, slow passing time that we perhaps know all too well. In English, the words chronology, chronicle, anachronism and chronic are all derived from *chronos*.

The Greeks invented a god named Chronos and gave him a serpentine shape and three heads – one a man, one a bull and one a lion. Regarded as destructive and all devouring, Chronos personified time. Fearing a prophecy that his own son would overthrow him, he swallowed each of his children as they were born. The Romans transformed the Greek god

Chronos into Saturn. Saturn also ate his children. In our lives, *chronos* can make us demented. We race against the god Chronos or Saturn and it is what ultimately kills us, eats us. The comedian Jerry Seinfeld says that 95% of life is killing time. Days and years are counted and regretted. I can too easily get caught in the habit of *chronos*. If each and every day my mind and my body dwell only in *chronos* time, it grinds me down.

How to cultivate *Kairos*/spaciousness

At the end of a recent PBS interview, Paula Zahn asked choreographer Bill T. Jones about the future, about where he thought the pendulum might be swinging. His answer was instructive. "Where is the pendulum swinging?" he asked.

> I don't know ladies and gentlemen but I will tell you this: It will swing and we will not know where it is swinging. Will we be ready? That is my last word: it's a question. How to get ready? How to have the youth educated, calm enough, clear in spirit. How to have the audience's eyes sophisticated enough, the critics open-minded enough, able to negotiate lots of different strands of investigation and to be humble enough to know when they don't know what they are looking at. *Will we be ready?*

Readiness seems to be one of the keys to unlocking the experience of both spaciousness and *kairos*. To wait, ready, like a hunter, the timing is everything. In order to develop the capacity to respond effectively to opportunities that arise and to also know when to hold back, I believe that the cultivation of *kairos* is crucial.

Just before the final chord of a Beethoven sonata, the virtuosic pianist Alfred Brendel often suspends his hands over the keyboard, silently asking the concert audience how long they will allow him to pause before he brings his hands down to play the final chord. Brendel is tempting the situation, playing with time and the expectations of the audience. The silence is filled with spaciousness and potential. In these instants, time seems to stop. *Kairos*.

Kairos is the alternative, the readiness to take advantage of changing circumstances. It is withheld from no one, but one must do the preparatory work to be in a position to perceive it. Because it is not "our" time, we do not own it and as such it cannot be controlled; it happens when it happens. It is necessary to cooperate with *kairos* rather than force it. Hunting and rehearsal are two examples of situations where *kairos* is crucial. Great comedic timing demands an intuitive sense of *kairos*, as does a musical improvisation. In these situations, one enters into a state in which timing is everything.

The state of readiness for opportunities to arise requires consciousness, vigilance and effort. To cultivate *kairos* I have to consciously stop, take a breath and check in on the quality of the moment rather than the running of the clock. When I practice T'ai Chi Ch'uan, my first gesture is to take off my watch and put it into a pocket. I do this because I do not want the constriction of a watchband. But I realize that it is a symbolic action as well: in the time set aside to practice, I remove *chronos* and *kairos* takes its place. One breath and then another breath and then the next. One. At. A. Time.

Kairos cannot be planned, and it certainly cannot be forced. The best I can do is to pay attention to the sort of things that lure it in my direction. The artist at work is in *kairos*. The child at play absorbed in a game, whether building a sand castle or making a daisy chain, is *kairos*; and so is lovemaking. It seems to me that the practice of the Viewpoints, an interval of consistant readiness and a state of potential, even in the midst of action, is *kairos*. Perhaps in *kairos* we become what we are called on to be as human beings, touching upon the wonder of creation.

Actors and spaciousness

An actor onstage, speaking a monologue in front of an audience, is undergoing more stress than an Olympic athlete in the midst of a high jump event, a fact established in scientific studies. Despite the immense pressure, the actor aims at a sense of effortlessness, even pleasure in the doing. Meanwhile she or he must be able to clearly differentiate one moment from the next and then the next and then the next. In order to succeed in this juggling act, the actor slows down to find spaciousness within the pressurized crisis of performance.

I saw George Bigot perform Richard II with the Théâtre du Soleil in Paris in 1981 directed by Ariane Mnouchkine. To me his performance was revelatory, wildly free, differentiated and unconventional. Intrigued, I stayed after the performance for a post-show discussion during which Bigot described the circuitous process that enabled him to play Richard II with such apparent spaciousness and abandon. A Théâtre du Soleil rehearsal period generally begins with a two-month workshop during which all of the actors engage in improvisation and experimentation. It is only after this that Mnouchkine decides upon the final casting. During the workshops Bigot felt completely free to play and improvise. But when Mnouchkine cast him as Richard II he froze. "How does a king walk?" he asked himself, "How does a king talk?" Seriously blocked, every move that he made onstage felt forced and artificial to him. Finally, after much struggle with the role, he realized that a young child, for example an eight-year-old boy, could play a powerful king with ease. This insight finally provided Bigot the permission to act the role of Richard II with great freedom and abandon. What the audience experienced as a portrayal of a powerful king was in fact George Bigot performing an eight-year-old boy playing a king. And yet his performance exuded clarity, majesty and expressivity. In order to find the spaciousness and ease necessary to play a king in the full authority of power, Bigot had to go through the back door. On the other side of that door, he found permission.

I met a Russian actress who said, "The job of the actor is to direct the role." Despite its simplicity, I find this trope practically revolutionary in our current theater environment. Too often actors wait for directors to tell them what to do and directors consequently assume that their job is to direct the actor's role. But ultimately, if you consider the totality, the director's job is not to direct the actor's role; rather, the director's job is to direct the *play*. Rather than suffocate the actor, the director should pay attention to the whole picture. While the director is occupied with directing the play, actors require space to consciously and intuitively direct their own roles. Each gives the other space. Like a hunter, always attentive to the whole, the director waits for the moment in which the arrangement of spatial and temporal issues begins to vibrate. And the actor is but a part of this arrangement.

In the theater, the art of the actor lies in his or her ability to invite a live audience on a journey in space and time and to differentiate each moment within the play repeatedly. Film and television, on the other hand, require the actor to be spontaneous, intimate and photogenic. That's it. In the hands of a film or television director and editor, actors' performances are regularly ripped apart and re-arranged into what feels rhythmically and semiotically satisfying. Unfortunately, film and television editing has unintentionally invaded the arena of the theater. Because in film the actor is only responsible for the bits and pieces of their "part," and because of a general confusion about the difference between acting for film and acting for theater, actors have largely relinquished their responsibility and agency in live theater by leaving it to the director to assemble their performances. Due to this confusion, actors in the theater have forfeited the responsibility for the whole arc of their role to the director. This has unfortunate repercussions for theater audiences, who want to grab the coattails of the actors and ride them through the entire play, from beginning to end.

Veteran acting teacher Steve Wangh developed an exercise that, he suggests, can teach an actor everything that they need to know about acting. Five or more actors enter the stage together, each with the task of grabbing and sustaining all of the audience's attention. Although this may seem to be an exercise in blatant narcissism and selfishness, in fact actors swiftly learn that being loud and obvious does not attract and maintain an audience's attention. To attract attention an actor must first concentrate their energy, intensely focus on one action at a time and find inner patience and spaciousness. Slowing down to intricately assemble a bicycle wheel or to study the fascinating shape of one's own moving finger or to intently watch another actor can, in turn, focus the audience. In addition to finding focus and inner spaciousness, an effective actor also chooses what to show and what to keep private. When an audience begins to suspect that there is more going on than what they can immediately see, that the actor is consciously not showing everything, their interest increases. Steve Wangh's exercise teaches actors the importance of clear focus, internal spaciousness and selective display.

Directors and spaciousness

I have devoted my life to directing, which I consider an art form. What makes directing an art? The *Dictionary Britannica* defines art as "the use of skill and imagination in the creation of aesthetic objects, environments, or experiences that can be shared with others." Directing requires exactly that: the conscious and unconscious, instinctive and technically informed shaping and arranging that stimulates and affects the emotions, the intellect and the senses of an audience.

Directing as a profession did not happen until relatively recently. In ancient Greece, the playwright was responsible for training the chorus, writing the music and staging his own plays. In medieval Europe, large-scale religious dramas and mystery plays required a pageant master to coordinate processions, crowd scenes and elaborate effects. Later, from the Renaissance through the nineteenth century, "actor-managers" chose repertory for a company, cast plays and oversaw the designs and production. The idea of a director as a necessary artistic component of the process did not occur until the early twentieth century.

Clearly, directing requires skill, taste and intuition. Intuition demands inner spaciousness. Despite the constant nagging tension of deadlines in the theater, spaciousness is a necessary ingredient in each stage of the process of bringing a project to fruition. Playwrights and designers require the freedom to experiment and search. Actors need leeway to find their character and trajectory. Part of a director's job is to provide spaciousness and permission for others, to allow colleagues to do their jobs. But a director requires spaciousness as well.

Personally and professionally I crave spaciousness. I long for enough space and time to cogitate, to roam around and to develop hunches around whatever project I am involved with. But spaciousness is hard to achieve. Life seems to conspire to keep it from me. All directors are faced with the great juggling act that defines their profession: the expectations, the wheeling and dealing, convincing potential producers and fundraisers that a project is worth their support, the tension of casting, the in-depth research and preparation, the countless discrete psychologies bearing down in the heat of a rehearsal, the skepticism of others, the rejection, the disagreement and even disbelief. All of these pressures are real. And yet, without cultivating the necessary spacious-ness in my own life, how can I walk into a rehearsal hall or design process and offer the requisite spaciousness to others?

My grandfather, Admiral Raymond Spruance, became Commander in Chief of the US Pacific Fleet during the Second World War and was generally credited as the brains behind the success of the Battle of Midway, which was considered to be the turning point of the war in the Pacific, as well as the Battle of the Philippine Sea. A calm and scholarly man whose demeanor did not draw personal attention although his skills did, he was notorious not only for his brilliance as a strategist, but also for his habit of falling asleep in the midst of crucial battles. Invari-ably would come a knock at his cabin door. "Admiral, a submarine has been hit by Japanese torpedoes." My grandfather would retort, "Why did you wake me up? We have been through this. We have a plan and everyone knows perfectly well what to do."

I often think of this story about my grandfather in relation to direct-ing theater. An actor does not stop a performance to ask the director what to do next. The planning, the strategy, the intentions have already been laid out and worked upon in rehearsal. When the audience enters the theater, the director's job, for the moment, is done.

Most directors are acquainted with the feeling of uselessness when rehearsals turn into previews and an audience arrives. Suddenly for the director there is simply nowhere to leave your jacket or bag. There is no space for you. Everyone else has their stations – the stage manager is in the booth and the actors in their dressing rooms. The director wanders around aimlessly looking for a place to leave their belongings. This sense of displacement is spiritual as well as it is practical. I complained repeatedly about this problem of displacement until Sue White, the production manager at New York Theatre Workshop where I was working at the time, hammered a nail into the wall of the box office and wrote underneath "Director's Hook." The practical problem was solved. The spiritual one was not.

But the problem of displacement is an interesting one. Ultimately, a theater director's job is to make her or himself useless. At first, in the process of any production, the director takes up a great deal of space, setting the sights for the creative team and describing the parameters. A director is a strategist and a juggler. Responsible for translating the world of the play into the languages of time and space, the director starts by developing strategic hunches and then proposing clear guidelines that actors, designers and other creative collaborators can use to find their way. And then, in rehearsal, the director serves as the actors' first audience. But at a crucial moment the director has to move away and allow the real audience to take their place. This adjustment can be painful and awkward but it is necessary. The intimate relationship between director and actors comes to an end and the director simply has to make space for something else. If I am still necessary after a show opens, then I have not properly handed the show over to the actors.

And yet a director can be useful after a play opens, especially with some distance, some time taken away, returning with fresh eyes and new perspectives. Even knowing that the director is present in the theater with an audience can give the actors a special heightened sense of being seen anew. For that brief moment in time and in space, the core community is re-established and the circular nature of feedback resumes.

Actors and directors: what is happening?

The space between actors and the director, which is to me a sacred arena, requires spaciousness but also critical incisiveness combined with immense patience. How can I allow spaciousness and yet also be present for the actors in practical ways?

What is happening? The director proposes a trajectory. The actor tries out ideas based upon the prompt. The director, as receiver, responds to the actor's attempts, both in the heat of the moment and after the fact, with notes. To use a funky analogy, the director is like a pH test strip for actors. Diagnostic litmus test strips are used to check the body to determine pH levels. The strips change color depending upon the acidic level of the person's urine. Likewise, the actor tries something out and metaphorically pees upon the director to determine what color the director becomes. To think of the director as litmus paper is to suggest that an actor can test his or her effectiveness by noticing the change in the constitution, or color, of the director, who is attending closely to the actor's actions. The actor can then make adjustments and try again, based upon the degree of success of his or her action upon the director.

As a director, my job is to stand in for a future audience. I find that micromanaging an actor rarely proves to be helpful. My attention must not be focused too directly upon one actor for very long. I give the actor space by placing her or him in my field of vision while I pay attention to the whole, to the relationships between the disparate components that make up the whole. Again, my job is to direct the play, not the actors. In the heat of the moment in rehearsal an actor can sense the quality of my attention and my own spaciousness, or lack of it, and can feel the excitement or energy that his or her attempt is generating in me. After the fact of rehearsal, of course, I give more thought-out notes, citing dramaturgical, psychological, spatial or temporal issues.

To consider the litmus metaphor further, it is necessary to examine the nature of the chemical reaction that is taking place between the actor and the director in rehearsal or between the actor and the audience in the heat of performance. The actor creates a strong inner life, a clear focus and well-defined actions, all the while taking care not to show too much. Despite the pressure of circumstance, the actor finds a way to be present in a way that the audience or the director cannot dismiss. I, the director, the future audience member, should feel that I would miss something if I looked away. A reverberation, a magnetic field is set up between the actors, the space and the audience.

Why is spaciousness necessary?

I directed Charles L. Mee's *Orestes* for SITI Company's inaugural season in 1992. We premiered the work in the mountainous region of Toga-mura, Japan at Tadashi Suzuki's International Arts Festival. Soon afterwards, both SITI and Suzuki's SCOT Company travelled to Saratoga Springs, New York, where each company would perform as part of SITI's first US season. I invited the SCOT Company to the dress rehearsal of *Orestes* in a 500-seat theater on the grounds of the Saratoga Performing Arts Center. The Japanese company, with Mr. Suzuki and his wife, Hiroko, arrived at the theater early and sat expectantly in the auditorium waiting for the run-through to begin, but a technical snafu prevented us from starting on time. Nervous and a little embarrassed, I clambered up to where the Japanese company was sitting and I proceeded to dance around and tell jokes in an attempt to entertain the group while they waited. Suddenly Hiroko turned and motioned sharply in my direction. "Shhh," she said, "the moments before a play begins are the most beautiful."

Hiroko put me in my place, confronting me with my own fear of nothing happening. I wonder if this is a typical American attitude – distrust of empty space and unfilled time? And yet how can anything new be created if we do not make space for it? I know that a great landscape painting has the power to catch the attentive viewer up in a brief caesura within the ephemeral rush of time and that actors in performance can change the time signature in the room by how they handle speaking and moving. I understand that an artist must be capable of stopping time and allowing for spaciousness. But now I also realize that to welcome the moments of stillness and quiet into my work, I must welcome and cultivate stillness and quiet into my own life. I must find the capacity to be still with nothing happening in order to realize that in fact something is always happening.

Silence does not exist, at least not as long as we are alive and breathing. Something is always moving. Something is always happening. But leaning in *towards* silence, welcoming the gaps and the dark places in between stillness and action, brings a great restorative reserve to our perceptual mechanisms and our sense of humanity. Much like mulch in gardening, the stinking dead leaves are transformed during the silence of winter into the fecund conditions that produce sweet tender bulbs. In the artistic process, the winter of quiet and invisibility is necessary for a burst of new life and expression to occur.

We are chock full of voices, all vying for attention – the voices of our parents, teachers, bullies and role models, all those who have filled us with inspiration, values, fears and prejudices. Their influence is both wonderful and horrifying and takes up a great deal of space. Their influence is wonderful because our dependence upon others is what gives life meaning. Wonderful because, like cattle, we are a herding species and our connection to others yields pleasure and meaning to our lives. Their influence can be horrifying because influences too easily become assumptions and preconceived notions and ideas. Assumptions are dead things and ultimately remove us from the fine tensile tissue of moment-to-moment living. Horrifying because when we hear too many voices we tend to get stuck, stranded upon the shores of too many opinions. The spaciousness that we require can be crowded out by too much noise.

Early in his career, before he co-founded the Guthrie Theater or became the executive director of Theater Communications Group (TCG), Peter Zeisler was choreographer Martha Graham's stage manager. He told me a story. One day, Martha Graham called Zeisler and asked him to be present at her home for a design meeting with the Japanese visual artist, Isamu Noguchi, who was to design Graham's next dance. As Zeisler described it, Noguchi arrived and sat down with Graham on a couch in her living room. He opened a briefcase, took out an egg and placed it upon the coffee table in front of them. After a long period of silence, Graham looked at Noguchi and said, "I see exactly what you mean." This marked the end of the design meeting. These two artists had successfully created the spaciousness for their collaboration. In contrast to *kairos*, *chronos* or measurement eats us alive. Literally. We die from *chronos*. It always ends up killing us. It takes away everything that we have and then eats us. When we break objects down into their parts and focus hard on the pieces, we are generally in *chronos*. Like dissection, this methodology works best when the subjects are dead.

On the other hand, I can shift to *kairos* when I concentrate on the space *around* the pieces, when I allow the space between things to matter more than the things themselves. When I think less about fiddling with particular objects and more about recognizing or influencing the patterns they create and the connections that they engender.

Recently my colleague, the director Brian Kulick, declared that life is moving faster. "Yes," I said in agreement. "Things do seem to be moving faster." "No, life does not *seem* to be moving faster, rather life really *is* moving faster," he said. "Yes," I said again, "life is getting faster." And again he repeated, "Life is *actually* getting faster." Brian is the first to admit to being fully part of the accelerated pace of humanity. He listens to podcasts when he is walking from one engagement to the next. In the attempt not to lose time, he said, he misses out on time.

I emailed Brian to ask for further explanation and he wrote back, "This escalation in time is in direct relation to our burgeoning technology where iPhones, iPads, Blackberries, etc. absorb all of our 'in between' and 'down time' to the point where there is no 'in between,' just differing levels of continual engagement. But these random minutes that happen while we wait for a train or a cup of coffee, or eat a pretzel and look at a building that we never noticed before, are all an essential part of the fabric of life: they give breadth and depth to our day; without them, the day careens onward with no time that is 'outside' of time. We need those 'outside' moments; they give us our sense of temporal proportion, our sense of balance."

Brian's words and sense of loss are well placed. To stare at the sky until you begin to sense patterns in the clouds brings a certain peace to the soul and the spaciousness that is necessary to be able to land fully in any particular moment.

When Hiroko Suzuki shhh-ed me in 1992 in Saratoga Springs before the run-through of *Orestes*, she made it clear that artists and audiences need to find the inner capacity to meet an event with spaciousness and a sense of possibility. Both life and art can prepare us for the openness that we need to bring ourselves to the unfolding moment. Can I walk out of my front door each morning and create enough space to see and experience the environment as freshly as if I were on vacation in a far-off land?

The body as barometer

The body as barometer is a simple notion. My body receives myriad impressions from multifarious sources, including temperature, patterns, noise, odor and color. These sensations and perceptions intertwine with my memories, associations, ingrained prejudices, long-term goals and learned responses. In this way, my own body, which is so wrapped up in and ultimately not separated from the world around it, can be easily overwhelmed. Fortunately, in a trope borrowed from Marshall McLuhan, who in turn borrowed it from International Business Machines (IBM), "information overload equals pattern recognition." My body can be the monitor. Simply by listening, by paying attention to the degree of my body's excitement and energy, or lack thereof, I can detect patterns. My body tells me what requires attention and what to ignore.

I call this "the goose-bump factor." One of the strongest and most useful signals that the body can generate are goose bumps, or what the French call, perhaps more poetically, *frisson du corps*. I have found that "the goose-bump factor" is useful when making important decisions, when deciding which path to take or while directing. When I feel a *frisson du corps*, I know that I should act. When I do not feel goose bumps, I do not. It is that simple.

I use "the goose-bump factor" when deciding whether or not to embark upon a particular new project or play. If the prospect of engagement with the subject or play gives me a *frisson du corps*, I know that I will be able to sustain the necessary energy and courage to meet all of the obstacles that will emerge in the process. If I do not feel goose bumps, I do not bother.

Using the body as barometer also helps me to handle criticism. If the criticism makes me angry, if it stirs my blood, I know that the criticism is useful and that I should pay attention. If I feel nothing, I know that the criticism is not helpful or relevant to what I am trying to do and I do nothing. The body, as barometer, works for me.

The balance of *chronos* and *kairos*

Perhaps the key to managing *chronos* and *kairos* is found in their balance. I have learned that if I handle *chronos* properly, then *kairos* can arise. If my objective in the theater is to elevate the quality of the time spent together, then perhaps attention to and management of *chronos* is the preparation for receiving *kairos*. Insuring a prompt start and end time of a rehearsal or performance and showing respect for everyone's *chronos* permits the assembled to savor the potential, the *kairos*, in each and every moment and allows for journeys to take off in unexpected directions. In rehearsal and in class I insist on beginning and ending exactly on time. If I had my way, performances would commence at precisely the appointed hour. I am not a temperamental director but stage managers know that I can become a bit nasty between 8:00 p.m. and 8:05 or whenever the performance is supposed to begin. "A play is like a soufflé," I complain, "and beginning late will deflate the event."

And yet, perhaps my solution for balancing *chronos* and *kairos* is cultural or Protestant or even military. At a theater festival in Bogota, Colombia, our production *Culture of Desire* was meant to commence at 8:00 p.m. The doors opened at 8:00, the audience entered leisurely, but our show did not begin until well past 9:00. Despite my nervousness about the late start, no one else seemed to mind and in fact the shared time amidst the audience was graceful and festive. The *kairos* commenced upon the occasion and chemistry of the audience's gathering. The circumstances were right for *kairos* in the context of the festival.

How is it possible to find spaciousness in the whirl of my day-to-day life and in my work? My task is to find stillness within motion. My task is to allow for the existence of *kairos*, which is a crossroads that intersects the linear passage of time. *Kairos* is pregnant time, the time of possibility, and seems to become the moments in the day, week and month, year or lifetime that defines me. *Kairos* is the right or opportune moment. How does the archer know when to release the arrow? *Kairos* is the time apart from the sequential time that we know and inhabit each day, a time when things of great magnitude or special significance happen. It is time outside of time, quality time, special time and crucial time. *Kairos* cannot be measured and yet it always leaves an impression, an impact. I cannot make it happen but I can create the conditions for it to happen and I must be ready to receive it.

Chapter 8

Empathy

> How else can we imagine living together without this ability to see beyond where we are, to find ourselves linked with others we have never directly known, and to understand that, in some abiding and urgent sense, we share a world?
>
> (Judith Butler, philosopher)

Most mothers are good at particular stages in their offspring's life but rarely for the entire time. My own mother was probably a great mother when I was a young child, but looking back she seemed to disconnect during my difficult teenage years. I struggled against what I felt to be her distance, intolerance and impatience.

But in the process of dying, she excelled once again in the art of motherhood.

Margaret Spruance Bogart was born into a Navy family. Her father, my grandfather, Admiral Raymond Spruance, is best known for commanding the Pacific Fleet during the Second World War, particularly during the Battle of Midway, a decisive turning-point victory over the Japanese Navy. He continued to command naval forces successfully throughout the course of the war and later served as the American ambassador to the Philippines. His hyper-intelligence and quick-thinking abilities earned him the nickname "electric brain."

Deeply curious, a lifelong reader and educated at Vassar College, my mother had an incisive intelligence, a quick mind and an uncanny ability to learn foreign languages. Following the Second World War she met my father, Gerard S. Bogart, a young naval officer studying at the Naval War College in Newport, Rhode Island, where my grandfather was president. Soon after they married, my parents were transferred to Warsaw and then to Berlin as part of the postwar scramble over ownership and influence in the Eastern-Bloc European countries. My older brother, David, was born in Berlin in 1949 during the Berlin Airlift. I was born in Newport, Rhode Island in 1951. Five years later, my younger brother, Del, was born in Tokyo, Japan.

From my infancy and until about the age of 12, my mother remained fully present, protective yet encouraging forays outside of her immediate sphere, providing me with an appetite for action and independence. Throughout those years I was always conscious of her presence, support and attention. She allowed space for growth and yet my brothers and I knew innately that she would be ready to catch any fall. As part of a Navy family we often lived by the ocean, by water. I remember my mother encouraging us to strike out into big surf alone and without fear. "Just try. Don't be afraid," she said. Through her trust in our abilities, she, in turn, instilled a sense of adventure in her little children.

Slowly this childhood paradise dissolved and was replaced by an ever-growing tension between my mother and me. Early on I became frustrated by the male hegemony of my Navy family. My brothers, because they were boys and expected to eventually become naval officers, were sent to first-rate private schools. For girls there were few expectations beyond becoming a Navy wife, and so I was sent to overcrowded, mediocre public schools. My mother seemed to think that this was the normal state of gender difference and expectations. And then there was the water. My father's idea of a family vacation was to step off whatever ship he was stationed on; we would all board a sailboat and sail out until land disappeared and stay there until he had to return to work. My brothers were given jobs to do on the boat. As boys they were taught to sail, fix motors and navigate. My mother cooked in the small galley and I was left with nothing to do but read. I grew to hate the confines of the boat and the water that surrounded us felt like a prison. Reading became my escape and welcome relief from what seemed to be an intolerable situation.

During my teenage years my mother and I struggled a great deal. We did not seem to understand one another and I resented her haughty attitude and what I felt to be her intolerance of my proclivities first for horses, then theater and then, as if to add insult to injury, hippie values and lifestyle. To this day I wonder if the apparent distance reflected a spike in her clandestine intake of alcohol. As a way to solve our apparent disjunction, I did my own distancing act. I began to crave financial and physical independence. I lied about my age in order to obtain summer employment during the high school years. The jobs, the travel to far-away places and my involvement in theater were the choices I made in order to distance myself from our struggle. I sensed that my activities were both a source of irritation for my mother and, at the same time, pride. The irritant between us may have had something to do with the fact that I was independent and active in ways that she had never allowed for herself. She chose the life of a Navy wife and I was off having a life of adventure and independence.

I began to direct plays while a student at Middletown High School in Rhode Island and dreamt of attending an excellent women's college and becoming a theater director. Unfortunately, after applying to Sarah Lawrence, Vassar and Bennington I was turned down from all of them. My mother was particularly distressed that her alma mater, Vassar College, had not accepted me. She held a grudge against the school for years afterwards by refusing to donate any money to the alumni fund. She just could not get past the fact that her beloved Vassar had turned down her only daughter.

I moved around a lot during my undergraduate years. Five years and four colleges later I graduated from Bard College and then moved to New York City to become a professional theater director. An added bonus of moving to Manhattan was the mistrust my parents harbored for any urban environment, especially New York City. Manhattan felt like a safe island far from the stress and pressure of family. I felt free on this island of iniquities.

Cancer brought my mother and me back together again. I was diagnosed with breast cancer at the age of 37. The doctors asked if there had been any history of breast cancer in my family. "No," I insisted, "there has been none." I chose to have the operation and begin recovery at my parents' home near Monterey, California, in a house near the Pacific Ocean that they had lived in since my father retired from the Navy, the house that my grandparents Spruance had purchased soon after the end of the Second World War. My parents were tender, worried and exceedingly present and generous with me during this traumatic time. After my treatment, I asked my mother if she had ever had a mammogram. "No," she said. I was adamant that she should have a mammogram as soon as possible. She did. The result: a detection of breast cancer in her left breast, the same side as my cancer. Like me, she underwent a modified radical mastectomy but the lymph node involvement was enough to require extensive chemotherapy. She lived for five more years before succumbing.

A couple of years after our rapprochement and before my mother's death, I began to teach at Columbia University, where I run the graduate directing program. One day I received a letter from Vassar College inquiring about my interest in leading their theater program. I called my mother immediately. When I told her about the inquiry from Vassar, she rejoiced. She was thrilled that the college that had turned me down, her very own alma mater, now wanted me to run their theater department. "You have to call them," she said. "You have to tell them that they turned you down!" She seemed both delighted and vindicated. A circle had somehow closed for her in a positive way. Perhaps the circle had closed for both of us. I felt her see me in a way that I had longed for: appreciated and valued.

The Christmas before my mother died, I spent several weeks with her in California. I am grateful for every moment that we spent together. Once a great hiker, by this time she could barely walk for ten minutes without collapsing in exhaustion. Nonetheless, we walked each and every day. Occasionally and uncharacteristically, my mother would take my arm for support. We drove together to see art movies that provoked long conversations. Ironically, it was the cancer that served as the catalyst that brought us back together. The crisis of limited time shifted our priorities and granted us a new closeness. Gone were the mysterious frustrations that had marked our relationship for so many years. The low-grade irritation was replaced by her genuine pride in me and her interest in and support for the life I had chosen. For my part I wanted to learn as much as I could about her life and experiences in the time remaining.

In early June of 1996, my mother telephoned from California with the news that she would probably live only for another six weeks. She wanted to see her three children together. I leapt on the very next plane from Albany, New York, near Saratoga Springs where SITI Company was in residence. I felt the tragedy of my mother's imminent death in my bones. I arrived in Monterey to find her weak but happy to see her children. Young at 76, my mother's intelligence, her mind, was sharp while her body was rapidly disintegrating. My brothers and I kept vigil that weekend around her bed. At one point she insisted that the three of us go off to nearby Monterey Harbor, where thousands of seals had recently and unexpectedly shown up, uncharacteristically beached upon the rocks near the middle of the town. Ours was a peculiar sibling excursion to visit the harbor. Thousands of seals had, for some mysterious reason, congregated upon the rocks near the harbor in downtown Monterey. Much to the puzzlement of marine biologists, the seals left their usual haunts on desolate rocks along the lonely California coastline to enter the crowded harbor. David, Del and I watched silently for a long time while the seals grouped and re-grouped, bleated and barked, frolicked and brawled, and young recalcitrant ones were dragged away by elder seals. In our sorrow and confusion about our own mother, the spectacle of the seals seemed to express a profound truth about families. Whether mammal, fish or reptile, all families make a similar progress through endless cycles of infancy, maturation, procreation, aging and death, over and over again. To this day my brothers and I have never discussed our silent journey, but I believe that the seals remain etched into our memories.

At the end of the weekend I entered my mother's bedroom to say goodbye. "I will return next weekend to see you again," I said. "No," she countered. I felt a physical shock at the emphatic word, "No." She continued, "I do not want you to sit around me as I fade away into a morphine haze. I want to say goodbye to you now. I do not want you to come back to California to see me again." I could not believe my ears. I protested. I argued that I should return, that I, her daughter, should be there with her in her final days. But my mother was unyielding. She knew exactly what she wanted and how she wanted her departure to occur. I left her to collect my bags. My body trembled. I did not understand. I gathered myself and returned to the bedroom and took a deep breath. I looked in her eyes and spoke slowly, "Thank you for being a great mother. I love you, goodbye." We kissed. The last thing my mother said to me before I left was, "Wish me luck."

Even though I spoke to my mother on the phone many times a day as she processed on her journey towards and into death, it was the opportunity to say goodbye in the full force of her presence, conscious and fully sentient, in that room together, that will remain with me for the rest of my life. My brother David, who lives with his family near Monterey, remained present at my mother's side, as did my father who, unable to accept the course of events, began to sink into early Alzheimer's.

I exited the plane in Albany, shattered but also slowly realizing that my mother was correct. I never would have said goodbye to her properly if she had not forced the brutal separation. As the wife of a naval officer she may not have had many choices but at the end she took the reins. She claimed her own life in the moments of her death. And in doing so she forced me not to be selfish or egotistical but rather to be empathetic to *her* situation, to put myself in her place.

My mother taught us many significant lessons in her dying. She became the embodiment of courage and independence. She demonstrated that in some pivotal issues we could consciously make our own choices. She showed us the force and clarity possible in the presence of one another. Her acute attention to her own dying taught me how I might pass that same threshold. And in the memories and recollections I hold of those final years, she continues to teach me the power of unmediated personal exchange.

Empathy is the act of taking other people's stories seriously.

(Kathryn Schulz, journalist, writer)

Israeli psychologist Daniel Kahneman proposes that we can think of ourselves as two separate beings. He distinguishes between the experiencing self and the remembering self. The experiencing self lives in the present moment. The remembering self keeps track of the past and creates stories from the experiences of the experiencing self. What we keep from our experiences becomes a story. There is a significant difference between the experience and the memory of the experience. I remember my mother now via the stories that I tell about her.

The capacity to see, to perceive the world through another's eyes, to empathize, is a vital sign of a civilized culture. Entering into the mindset of another person can alter the brain's synaptic pathways. Our morality is grounded in the ability to empathize with others. Empathy is powerful. The act of empathizing with others alters perspective.

Audiences are attracted to the theater for the direct visceral experience as well as for the anticipated emotions and, consequently, the memories. New memories are added to existing ones. What creates memory? Experience and sensation become memory via emotion. The more emotion that is generated in the heat of an experience, the more likely that the memory will "stick." Emotion seals memory. The stronger the emotion, the more accessible the memory is. I try to make theater that feels to me both visceral and exciting in the moment, but that also might create pathways to new and lasting memories. I hope that if it happens in me, it will happen with audiences as well.

Memory is a protein that forms and "sticks" in the brain in the heat of experience. For example, my initial experience in the theater at the age of 15 was a highly emotional encounter. The experience led me to choose the theater as a profession. I can still remember this experience easily. To access this memory now, a particular synaptic path must be created that leads to the original protein. The memory is a new creation all over again.

> Logic will never change perception or emotion.
>
> (Edward de Bono, physician, consultant)

The brain, which craves novelty, responds best to narrative. And narrative, in turn, stimulates empathy and emotion. Stories are particularly powerful because they engage the entire brain. Facts, on the other hand, only stimulate narrow aspects and smaller parts of the brain. Empathy instigated through stories has the potential to make strong, visceral impressions, which in turn can transform attitudes, which then can alter behavior.

It is nearly impossible to convince anyone of anything via facts, charts, numbers or even documented proof because the brain does not respond much to facts alone. Confronted with facts, even powerful facts combined with persuasive arguments, people do not generally change their opinions. Evidence and even proof can impress people in the short term but they rarely engender lasting change. But when facts are contextualized within stories, the effect is exponential. People's minds can be deeply affected through the alchemy of emotion plus empathy in the heat of a story. With a story, the message will stick.

The most successful non-fiction, including essays, documentaries and news reportage, is presented in narrative form using the conventions of fiction. The Bible is essentially a collection of stories and parables that stick in the mind and serve to provoke questions, challenge assumptions and expand the empathic response. Translating complex, new scientific discoveries into understandable concepts for the general public requires great storytelling. The physicist Brian Greene is currently helping us to understand string theory and parallel universes. Sigmund Freud was a great storyteller, as was Carl Sagan. Their own profound understanding, conjoined with their ability to communicate with others, gave the general public the courage to enter new scientific paradigms.

> To live well as human beings, we need to be moved in good ways by emotions that are about others.
>
> (Paul Woodruff, philosopher)

An article in *The New York Times* recounted the story of young Americans who, in sympathy with their Holocaust-survivor grandparents, had the same numbers tattooed onto their own arms that the Nazis had tattooed onto their grandparents' bodies. The shared tattoos are acts of physical memory, of loyalty and of empathy that link the generations and their histories, one to the other. Besides providing the young tattooed person with a sense of solidarity with those who were in the camps, their actions transcend the fact of the prison camps and make history more emotional and personal in the present.

> This obsession with the self is of course exactly the opposite of centuries of spiritual seeking, which were all about how to escape the self. How can we finally annihilate this thing called the self, and literally transcend it?
>
> (Peter Sellars, theater and opera director)

My dedication to the theater is unequivocally related to emotion, feeling and empathy. And yet, the theater is a complex medium and the creation of empathy is not as simple as the actor who says, "If I feel it, they will feel it." Audiences rarely feel empathy for a character by watching the actor feel that emotion. The actor does not get drunk to show drunkenness. The misguided notion that the actor and the audience feel the same sensations at the same time leads to a solipsistic approach to acting by the actor and easy dismissal of the actor by the audience.

A scholar watching a run-through of *Room*, a one-woman show based upon the writings of Virginia Woolf, was overcome with emotion at a particular point in the play. Later he interviewed the actress, Ellen Lauren, and asked her what she was thinking about during this specific section of the play. Ellen responded, "I was counting." Due to the intricate choreography and precise musical cues in the scene, Ellen found it necessary to count. The scholar was appalled. He could not believe that Ellen was counting while he felt such strong emotions and empathy for the character. But in fact, the actor was busy, engaged in setting up the necessary conditions for the audience's empathic response.

It is easy to create a moment on stage where everyone in the audience feels the same thing. But what I find much more interesting and challenging is to stage moments in which everyone experiences different associations and feelings. For example, I weep when I see a film in which a boy runs across a field towards his missing dog. I burst into tears at some advertisements. I get goose bumps from a high-jump feat. Feeling and emotion can be easily misused, manipulated and abused. On the contrary, it requires far more technique and savvy to create a moment where everyone in the theater is allowed a different response. If I want to treat the theater as an art form rather than advertising, I have to create space for diverse emotional and empathic experiences.

Pay attention to the cracks because that's where the light gets in.
(Leonard Cohen, singer, songwriter)

Despite the fact that I share most theater people's passionate interest in and curiosity about feeling and empathy, I nonetheless avoid addressing the subject too directly in the process of a rehearsal. Feeling and empathy is a byproduct of a precise arrangement of circumstances. When an actor forces the issue of feeling and empathy, she or he will miss it.

Anyone who wants to see a solar eclipse knows that looking directly at the sun is dangerous for the eyes. To witness the eclipse, one gazes to the side or looks at the reflection of the eclipse on a piece of cardboard. And yet, looking to the side is not the point, the cardboard is not the point; rather, the point is to experience the sun. In a similar sense, in a rehearsal, the fact that we share a passionate interest in empathy and feeling is precisely why we do not head directly at it. Attempting to manufacture emotion and feeling leads to cheap results. Instead, I tend to concentrate on precise details and technical points that come up, not because I am so fascinated by those things, but rather because I am trying to set up the circumstances in which feeling and empathy can occur.

If we want to survive, we must understand the actions of others. Furthermore, without action understanding, social organization is impossible. In the case of humans, there is another faculty that depends on the observation of others' actions: imitation learning. Unlike most species, we are able to learn by imitation, and this faculty is at the basis of human culture.

(Giacomo Rizzolatti, neurophysiologist)

Recent discoveries in neuroscience have thrown down the gauntlet to those of us in the theater who think seriously about the real effect of an actor's action upon the nervous system of an audience member.

In the 1990s, a group of Italian neuroscientists noticed that identical nerve cells discharged both when a monkey performs a specific action and when it observes another monkey performing that action. The researchers dubbed these newly discovered neurons *mirror neurons* because of the way they apparently mirrored an observed action in the monkey's brain. A monkey grabs a peanut and the monkey watching activates the same synaptic pathways. Both monkeys are *doing*. One monkey is visibly making an action; the other monkey is *restraining* from making the exact same action.

Of course it turns out that humans have mirror neurons too. The act of watching is not simply psychological interpretation or conjecture; rather, the act of watching is physical and energetic. The observation of a goal-oriented action triggers the identical synaptic activity in the observer as in the person who is generating the action. Attentive watching charges our bodies with electric currents. The mirror neuron activity creates a simulation of the activity being observed in the observer's brain, and in this way the observer gains a deeper understanding of a particular movement through actual physical simulation and stimulation.

Mirror neurons are the cells that allow us to understand one another by creating a meaningful link between the self and others by dissolving the boundaries between us. When mirror neurons are activated, people feel empathy. And empathy is the baseline of the theater experience and the unspoken contract between actor and audience. When Hedda Gabler lifts her pistol, I feel her spooky action from the distance of where I sit and I take it personally.

In 2004 a team of British neuroscientists conducted an experiment with two separate groups: dancers from London's Royal Ballet and experts in capoeira, a Brazilian martial arts form known for its physical rigor and acrobatic feats. Both groups watched videos of ballet or capoeira while hooked up to fMRI scanners. The mirror neuron system showed far more activity in individuals watching the discipline in which he or she was trained. The mirror neurons for capoeira experts watching capoeira were more activated than when watching ballet. The mirror neurons of the ballet dancers fired more when they watched ballet than when they watched capoeira. This demonstrates how a familiarity with the observed action stimulates more intensity and imagination than the less familiar action.

And this has everything to do with the theater. For your mirror neurons to fire, you have to be familiar with the action that you are observing. Theater is the art form that most resembles daily life. Actors walk, sit, speak, pick up a teacup, throw a book, kiss, shake hands or jump over a puddle. An audience member's own motor control cortex is more excited when seeing people doing moves that they *can* do than when seeing those they cannot do. Unlike watching virtuosic dance or looking at an abstract expressionist painting, the mirror neurons of a theater audience respond wildly to the action found in a play because of its familiarity. Add to this the human capacity to read intentions, another function of the mirror neuron system in humans, and the effect is exponential. And all of this happens in the unmediated live space between actors and audience in a theater.

Seeing is a process of projecting what you expect to happen and then matching your experience, your prejudice and your expectations with what is out there in the world. Matching observation with action is an active process. The system of mirror neurons embodies this principle. Celebrated neuroscientist Antonio Damasio describes mirror neurons as "puppet masters, pulling the strings of various memories."

In the theater when fully engaged, the audience does not passively watch what is happening; rather, the audience is active, neurons firing. The actors are a group of people doing (manifesting action) and the audience is a group of people watching (restraining from that same action). The audience is learning the action but ultimately is also restraining from actually doing the observed action. But this restraint is also a kind of action.

The activation of the mirror circuits on both sides of the footlights provides the observer with a real experience of empathy for the observed action and for the actor. The focused action in the body of the actor is transmitted to the neuronal system of each audience member. The observed action is literally being mapped onto the motor system of the observer. It is a physiological phenomenon. The audience's capacity for empathy, imitation, action understanding and intention understanding are all linked to this action in restraint. The mirror neuron system helps us to translate what we see in order to relate to the world better.

Scientists have found that the mirror areas, in addition to action understanding, also mediate the discernment of others' intentions. In our daily lives, we are constantly exposed to the actions of others. We are not only able to describe these actions, understand what they mean and predict their consequences, but we can also attribute intentions to the doer. In the theater we exercise these skills within the combination of the fiction of the play and the reality of the actors' actions. We see Hedda Gabler pick up a pistol. We recognize *that* she is picking up a pistol and we can infer *why* she is doing so. Is she is going to put it away safely, is she just toying with it or is she going to shoot herself?

If action is the central trope of the theater and it delivers the experience, it follows that our task in the theater is to make sure that the actions executed onstage are clear, precise and focused. Clear, focused action is more powerful and effective than fuzzy, imprecise action. The audience is a musical instrument being played upon by the actors. Clear actions are literally more invigorating to the nervous system of the audience than inexactitude, which saps the audience's energy.

> The art of theater is not entirely up to the performers. Part of my job in the audience is to be the kind of person who can be rewarded by watching such a performance.
>
> (Paul Woodruff, philosopher)

Empathy requires an investment of time, of single-minded concentration and of imagination. To reap the benefits of empathy, we must allow ourselves to be altered by the investment. Stories only succeed when we consent to suspend disbelief. Relationships require of us something similar: the ability to let go of our own worldview long enough to be intrigued and moved by someone else's.

At a panel discussion about "the necessity of theater" at the Cherry Lane Theater, a young person in the audience stated that she and her friends do not like going to the theater because they do not want to spend two hours out of contact with their friends. Her statement, to me, is counter-intuitive. I believe that two hours of concentration is healthy for the brain, for the emotions and, dare I say, for the soul. If you do not give yourself the gift of experiencing an enhanced vision of life through the prism of art, you are missing out. Perhaps single-minded concentration is necessary to balance the mad onslaught of our present culture's omnipresent diversion. The theater offers a site of communion and mutual concentration precisely *because* one is out of contact with the outside day-to-day world.

The British director John Doyle said that in rehearsal he demands that everyone shut down all laptops and phones. At first, he said, the stage managers are the most upset by his request. Stage managers generally take down blocking on their computers, and being online in rehearsal also means being in contact with the theater's administration as well as the outside world. Doyle assures the stage managers that whatever blocking they record would change anyway. Instead, all he asks of them is to simply be present and pay attention.

Over the past several years, computers have become a dominating presence in my own rehearsals. In a slow moment in rehearsal, the stage manager, who often is also simultaneously the company manager, may be making plane reservations for the actors for an upcoming tour. The designers are able to be in the room with us for the entire rehearsal process *only* because they are concurrently electronically present at other rehearsals around the city, around the country or even around the world. If they were not able to surf, text, iChat or email, they would probably not be able to be in the room with us as much as they are. A designer's livelihood depends upon being able to design multiple shows simultaneously.

But I wonder about the toll, about the fact that we are less and less *truly* in the same room together, all concentrating on the same single event of unfolding by the actors on the stage. Am I a Luddite? Am I negating the glorious accessibility of information that I enjoy enormously in my day-to-day existence? I am torn. I feel split.

I do not think that I am alone in my difficulty to keep up with the massive deluge of information that is available at any instant of the day or night. Nicolas Carr's *The Shallows: What the Internet Is Doing to Our Brains* suggests that our brains are being altered radically by new technologies. How we flip from one piece of information to the next, cross-indexing and jumping, multitasking and juggling, is having a severe toll on our overall ability to concentrate on one thing for an extended period of time. I have too much music on my iPod. I have lost track of what moved me the first time I heard a piece of music. My memory is overtaxed. I listen to a galvanizing track and then forget about it because I am afraid that I am missing something new on my eMusic account. But music is just the tip of the iceberg.

> Emotion is the chief source of becoming conscious.
>
> (Carl Jung, psychiatrist)

Patti Smith's beautiful book *Just Kids* traces her early years in New York with her closest friend and sometimes lover, the photographer Robert Mapplethorpe. The book offers a gorgeous ride through the Manhattan landscape of the late 1960s and early 1970s. I am struck by the difference between how Patti and Robert absorbed new information in those days and how we currently receive novelty and information in our present techno climate.

Often penniless and living in bare, unheated rooms, with very little to eat, Patti and Robert were voracious for poetry, visual art, music and literature. When one of them had saved enough money, they would purchase a record or a book. Together they huddled around the book or the record and listened to it or looked at it for weeks. Savoring the new influence, inevitably they were transformed by the time they spent with it. Their interaction was slow and deep.

Looking back at the days before Google and YouTube, iTunes and Amazon, Skype and text messaging, Facebook, Tumbler and Twitter, threads and RSS, I remember the preciousness and slowness of new acquisitions and new influences that came from either books, records or conversations or just from someone pointing in a direction and saying, "You should check this out." These acquisitions involved sweat and effort.

The market culture and its manufactured desires and materialistic promises have failed miserably. The unregulated markets resulted in a ravaged landscape of despair. The myth of economic progress as the answer to our baseline problems is simply not true. What else can there be? In this uncertain and cataclysmic climate, the creative impulse and the art experience is essential. In art we find a direction and the theater remains a highly effective site of fellow feeling. To create significant change in one's perception of the world, it is necessary to engage in emotional journeys of empathy and narrative that help us to participate in the world with others.

The steps that we take in order to enter deeply and emotionally into the lives and narratives of others create empathic journeys. We emerge from these journeys freed for a time from the prison of our own habitual worldview. The intimacy with and proximity to alternate experiences of reality do nothing less than offer us insight into the parallel universes of other lives. These journeys remind us that, in truth, we know little and can learn much.

Chapter 9

Collaboration

> I am interested in the actor because he is a fellow human being ... which means my encounter with a person other than myself, the feeling, the contact, the sense of mutual comprehension created by the fact that we are both opening ourselves to another human being, that we are trying to understand him and thus overcome our solitude.
>
> (Jerzy Grotowski, theater director)

Collaboration is notoriously tricky. Many respected theater artists insist that true collaboration is impossible. I heard a radio interview with the director Richard Foreman who was, at the time, in the midst of rehearsals for a production with writer Kathy Acker and visual artist David Salle. Asked about the collaboration he exclaimed "Collaboration? This is not a collaboration, this is a collision!"

The trouble is generally ego. When a dramaturg proposes a directorial idea or an actor proposes a design idea or a stage manager proposes an acting idea, egos get ruffled. We all know the feeling. "Hey, that's my territory! I'm the one who is supposed to be paying attention to that. Get out of my territory!"

The default setting for the human brain is fear, anxiety and the desire to be certain, none of which are helpful in the collaborative process. The propensity towards fear, anxiety and the desire to be certain is largely due to the way that the human brain developed in the dangerous and warlike environment of the ancient world. But once food, safety and shelter are established, it is possible to use the brain differently, capitalizing on its elasticity and our capacity to think and act differently. Particularly for artistic or scientific innovation, the mind must bypass habit in order to function in its splendid multiplicity. It is possible to sidestep the fear and safety impulses of the ancient brain and revel in the brain's ability to be flexible. Only with these adjustments is cross-disciplinary collaboration possible.

Active vs. passive culture

The process of collaboration is a road littered with real and tangible obstacles. Passivity is one of the most predominant problems because collaboration is too often misunderstood as agreement. But collaboration is emphatically not agreement. With too much agreement, too little happens. "The disease of agreement" engenders passivity and even worse passive aggression. Passivity is a disease protracted by assumptions about the need to act in harmony with others. In the rehearsal hall, rather than making a bold stroke on the blank canvas, an actor waits for a director's instructions. In the theater, an audience sits back and refuses to participate in the event of a performance.

Director Jerzy Grotowski's very public frustration with the passive nature of audiences in the theater is where I first encountered the words "active and passive culture." Eventually, in the mid 1970s, the endemic passive nature of audiences drove him to abandon traditional notions of theater, with its division of actors (active) and spectators (passive). Aiming to overcome passivity, Grotowski proposed "participatory theater" in which people from outside the theater, rather than simply observing staged productions, participated in experiences prepared by "leaders." These "para-theatrical experiments" later developed into phases that Grotowski labeled Theater of Sources, Objective Drama and Art as Vehicle. For Grotowski, the guiding principle of active culture was shared participation in the creative process by everyone present. He repositioned his theater to be an encounter between people rather than a show put on by one group for another.

Deeply influenced by Grotowski, I wondered how, in my own work, to encourage active rather than passive culture in the audience as well as active culture in the rehearsal hall. One of the most helpful tools for encouraging active culture in rehearsal is, for me, the Viewpoints, which requires actors to make intuitive decisions about the composition of space and time at each and every moment. Once actors have been introduced to the Viewpoints, the conventional atmosphere of the rehearsal hall transforms into an active culture. The director sets up certain parameters and then the actors begin to make choices without waiting for the director to tell them what to do.

Because the bedrock of SITI Company is collaboration, passivity in rehearsal has never been an issue. But I am often asked how to work with people who have either not trained in the Viewpoints or who bring a passive attitude to the rehearsal hall. The first thing to do, I propose, is to ask them, "What do you think?" And then say, "Show me."

The opera world is notoriously fraught with obstacles. Severe limitations caused by tight union rules, great financial cost and centuries of inbred assumptions and restrictions tend to generate a passive and seemingly inflexible culture on both sides of the proscenium. And yet, I find working in opera energizing and transformative. As a director, I enjoy the process of endeavoring to convert the tendencies of a passive culture into an active one in the context of an opera production. The results can be rewarding.

In 2001 at New York City Opera I directed a new opera entitled *Lilith*, composed by Deborah Drattell with a libretto by David Steven Cohen. In addition to the lead singers, *Lilith* has a substantial male chorus. Often mistreated and underappreciated in the opera world, choruses are notoriously brittle, resistant and suspect of any participation in active culture. And yet in opera the chorus often provides the solution to creating a compelling stage world. Having directed before at New York City Opera, I knew what lay ahead. On the first day of rehearsal, confident that sharing the Viewpoints would make the staging more collaborative and efficient, I asked the chorus men if they would be willing to take their shoes off for a half hour. "We do not take off our shoes," said the appointed representative of the men's chorus. "All right," I said, "I understand." Even with their shoes on I did manage to share some of the basic principles of the Viewpoints and the chorus seemed surprised but curious about this seemingly non-goal-oriented activity. The next day we began the process of staging the opera. At one point, I walked up to the chorus representative and asked him whether it would be funnier for all the men to tip their chairs on measure 78 or on measure 84. He seemed quite shocked to be asked. "You are the director," he said. "Yes," I responded, "But music is your lifetime occupation and you know much more about it than I do. I just wonder if it would be funnier to tip the chairs on measure 78 or 84." The man looked uncomfortably around at his colleagues. "Well," he said slowly, "actually the funniest moment to tip the chair would be on measure 91." "Gentlemen!" I said, "Let's all tip the chairs together on measure 91." And slowly the ice began to melt. "Ms. Bogart," a member of the chorus would shout out, "we all think that the moment for us to stand together should happen on measure 102." Things seemed to be getting better until one day the chorus decided that I was assigning them too many physical cues. "No problem," I said. Several days later, after some very lively chorus rehearsals, I arrived in the rehearsal hall where the chorus representative informed me that the chorus had met and voted for more cues. And so the process became increasingly collaborative. The atmosphere became jovial; jokes were mixed with the hard work of staging a massive opera. After rehearsals the chorus invited the members of SITI Company, who were also involved with the production, to a nearby bar/restaurant where they regaled us with stories of nightmare productions and abusive directors. But the most significant aspect of our shared active culture was what happened in performance. The men were powerful, present and vulnerable as they moved and sang on the stage. And they were proud of what we had accomplished together. They felt, I believe, ownership. Even from the distance of the back of the two-thousand-seat theater, I believe that the audience could feel the chorus's remarkable collective presence and contribution to the whole.

I also directed Drattell's *Nicolas and Alexandra* at the Los Angeles Opera. On the day of the final dress rehearsal, the production manager asked to speak with me. A tough, smart and capable woman and always strict about union rules and deadlines, she could be quite abrasive. Generally she intimidated me with her no-nonsense attitude. She took me off into a darkish corner backstage and I braced myself for the worst. "I just want to thank you," she began, but then her voice trembled a little, "because working with you reminded me of why I got into opera in the first place."

In addition to active culture in rehearsal, I believe that it is possible to encourage active culture in the audience as well. My job as a director is to create space for the audience's imagination and participation. What is *not* shown on stage is often more important than what *is* shown. There should be breathing space, imaginative space and associative space for the audience's creative participation with what is happening onstage. A set should suggest rather than describe a place and the audience constructs the rest in their imagination. An actor or singer's epigrammatic gestures, movements and actions express rather than define. The audience completes the stage picture.

Playwrights too can engender active culture in audiences. Charles Mee, Sarah Kane, Suzan Lori-Parks and other contemporary play-wrights create open texts that require audiences to become active co-writers. These playwrights ask audiences to be willing to tolerate gaps and suspend the task of meaning-making. No longer simply filling in the conventional gaps in dramatic narrative, the spectators are invited to become active eyewitnesses reflecting their own meaning-making into the event.

Windows

As a young director during the late 1970s in New York City, still finding my way in the performance and art scene, I had the extreme good fortune to meet the choreographer Mary Overlie. We were both teaching at New York University's new Experimental Theatre Wing and together we collaborated on several productions. She introduced me to what she then called the Six Viewpoints, an approach to improvisation that rocked my entire world. At the time, the conventional New York theater scene did little to excite my imagination. But the dance and visual art world teemed with innovation, experimentation and radical ideas. Mary Overlie was very much part of this downtown scene and I recognized how her exceptionally practical technique could enable and empower performers to generate exciting work together efficiently and collaboratively. The method opened my imagination to innumerable possibilities about how to activate the creative process with actors in rehearsal. Over the ensuing years, I adapted Mary's ideas for my own investigations and artistic evolution. Mary's Viewpoints provide a logical way to examine, analyze and create dances. My direction with the Viewpoints is considered practical for creating staging with actors. What excited me most was that the Viewpoints provide a training that places the actor at the center of the creative process.

Mary told me that early on she had considered calling the Viewpoints "Windows." I understood immediately. Look at a specific theatrical moment through the *window* of space. Look at the same moment through the *window* of shape. Look at the moment through the *window* of story or the *window* of time. The specific window through which we look determines how we look and what we are looking for; it defines our particular experience of the moment.

Mary's choice of the word "Windows" reminded me of the architecture of a peep show. In midtown Manhattan in the days before Times Square was transformed into a theme park, 42nd Street was littered with adult bookstores, topless bars, strip clubs and peep shows. As a part of research for a play about the seedy world of strip joints, I visited a peep show on the corner of Eighth Avenue and 42nd Street. I entered nervously into one of the booths that surrounded the circular performance space, put a quarter into a slot, and a window shade opened revealing a scantily clad woman on a raised platform in the middle of the circle of booths. I felt uncomfortable but also intrigued. I thought of the other people, probably men, each with very different intentions than mine, sitting in their own booths, with their own view of the woman's shape and movements. Perhaps the architecture of a peep show is a useful image in considering the way we approach different aspects of a play's development and also how we think about collaboration.

Each member of a collaborative team views the production from a separate booth and through a different window. There is a director window, a playwright window, a dramaturgical window, an actor window, a set design window, a lighting design window, a sound design window, a producer window and so on. Each artist looks at the very same event through a vastly different lens. For the best results, every moment of the play is examined with clarity through all of the different windows. Each window demands different skills and abilities.

Perhaps it is helpful to imagine that there is no such *person* as a director, no such *person* as a dramaturg, no such *person* as an actor, playwright or designer. Perhaps rather than specific people, think of these jobs as windows through which any member of the collaborative team can approach the shared effort. In thinking this way, the contributions of others may be less threatening.

For most of my life I have felt great passion for and interest in the profession of directing. I have studied and continue to study how to best look at a play through the lens, or window, of a director. But I do not feel threatened if someone else looks through my window. In fact, I know that at times it is essential to the process that I move away from my own window and look for a time through the dramaturgical window or the design window or the actor window. The views of the play through each window are radically different. And I know that it is also advantageous for my colleagues to do the same. Sound designer Darron West often steps into my proverbial booth, looks at the play through the director window and makes useful observations. Actors are also welcome to step into my booth.

An actor spends his or her entire life training to meet a live audience. A playwright faces the predicament of the blank page and then forges into battle to make something out of nothing. As a director, I provide the litmus test for an actor's attempts at expression in rehearsal. I am the first audience. But this does not mean that from time to time the roles cannot be fluid. I do not have to identify with my role so inflexibly that I cannot step away from the director booth and allow another person to step in and look at the play from the director's point of view. In true collaboration, all of these lenses or windows are necessary in the realization of a play.

The Taoists say, "Be round on the outside and square on the inside," which means be generous, respectful and civil on the outside but on the inside know exactly what you think and feel at all times. A director who spends time controlling the rehearsal in superficial ways, a director who is territorial and inflexible is not a strong director. To collaborate one needs a strong core and a supple and flexible exterior. Imagine steel wrapped in cotton. While it is true that the director is the person who makes the final decisions about how the play is put together, this aspect of control and power can be negotiated in various ways. If all of the collaborators genuinely feel the freedom to breathe and roam around, taking breaks from the relentless points of view of their own disciplines, they will ultimately contribute more and feel more ownership in the process and the project.

Why collaborate?

Often, even with the best intentions, collaborations fail. Japanese director Tadashi Suzuki once said, "International cultural exchange is impossible, therefore we must try." In a similar spirit, perhaps, true collaboration is impossible. But the effort can be tremendously fruitful.

I did not start out expecting to find a group of like-minded collaborators like SITI Company. It took years to arrive at an ensemble. Allow me to share an idea: you are in a room. Some people come into that room. You make a play together and then those people leave and you are alone again. After a while some new people come into the room. You make another play together and then *they* leave and you are alone again. After a while some other new people come into the room and you make a new play with them and then they leave as well and you are alone again. After a while some new people come into the room and you make yet another play together. But this time one person stays and now there are two. After a while some new people come into the room and you all make a play together. Most of them leave but two more people stay and now you are four. And so it goes. Slowly the room fills with collaborators. You did not set out to find those people; they are simply the people who decided to stay.

After 20 years with SITI Company, largely working with the same actors and designers, I now realize the full extent to which we have grown together. We are increasingly able to collaborate with one another. The accumulation of sustained collective effort has multiplied the skills of the actors and increased their appetite to climb ever higher mountains. The depths of this truth arrived full force during a pick-up rehearsal for the play *Death and the Ploughman*.

Originally written in 1401 in Bohemia by Johannes von Saaz and adapted by the contemporary Irish writer Michael West, the play *Death and the Ploughman* is a battle of logic and passion about why we live and why ultimately we must also die, a debate that many scholars insist marked the end of the Middle Ages and the launch of the Renaissance. When I first heard the text, I found it to be the most profound meditation about living, dying and living with grief that I had ever encountered. I decided to find a way to stage the play, the debate, with SITI Company. We premiered *Death and the Ploughman* in 2004 at the Wexner Center in Columbus, Ohio and we continue to tour it widely. The production, which features three SITI Company actors, Will Bond, Ellen Lauren and Stephen Webber, is perhaps the most challenging play for actors that I have ever directed.

On the first day of rehearsal for *Death and the Ploughman*, as we contemplated the complex and emotional issues of the play, Bondo, as we informally call Will Bond, who plays the Ploughman, asked me to provide him with an impossible acting task so that he would not have to think about the enormity of his task to speak such profound text and embody such grief and rage. The Ploughman, a man in the depths of grief after his beloved wife dies in childbirth, meets with Death to plead his case for the return of his loved one. I thought about Bondo's request overnight and came back to rehearsal the next day with a proposal. The play occurs in 32 scenes or what, in the spirit of the medieval triptych nature of the play, we call "panels." What if for every one of the 32 panels each actor would create 32 discrete movements? If each actor were to invent 32 moves for each of the 32 panels, the result would be 3,072 disparate moves executed all within the play's short duration of an hour and 20 minutes. The actors agreed and we began to create what became a dense, complicated and elaborate staging. The rigor of the movement combined with the density of the philosophical text required great physical virtuosity and real ensemble cooperation. But the difficulty must never be apparent to the audience; rather, the performances should exude ease and simplicity. The task was Herculean.

Now, many years after its premiere, performing *Death and the Ploughman* does not get any easier, especially as we are all growing older. The challenge is both gratifying and daunting but what became clear to me during the pick-up rehearsal is that all of us, actors, designers and technicians, are gradually getting better at what we do. We have learned from one another over time to be more courageous, truthful and generous. The trust that we share is the result of the many years of collaboration that has consistently tested our limits. And this just may be reason enough to sustain collaboration over a long period of time.

In a speech to graduating students at Columbia School of the Arts, the composer David Byrne had a two-part message. First, choose yourself. "Too many people wait to be chosen," he said. "Do not wait. Choose yourself." Second, cross-disciplinary collaboration is the only sustaining hope for the field of performance. He encouraged the newly minted MFAs to collaborate with others and be altered by the experience of doing so. His own career provides a vibrant example. He has collaborated with Brian Eno, St. Vincent, Fatboy Slim, Dirty Projectors, Caetano Veloso, Selena, Marisa Monte and Maximum Balloon. He works regularly with choreographer Annie B. Parsons and more recently with theater director Alex Timbers.

I realize how essential it is for SITI Company and for me to continue to collaborate with artists from different disciplines. In recent years we have gravitated towards collaborations with visual artist Ann Hamilton, choreographer Bill T. Jones and his company, the Martha Graham Dance Company, composer Julia Wolfe and the Bang on a Can All Stars. For me, being in the room – collaborating – with people who offer diverse perspectives is key to my evolution. It is in the gap between what I think I know and the reality of all that I do not know that transformation occurs.

Four steps

Anthropologist Angeles Arrien proposed four rules for living:

1 Show up.
2 Pay attention.
3 Tell the truth.
4 Don't be attached to the results.

These four rules are also applicable to the art of collaboration. But the simple words that constitute these rules are deceptively difficult to actualize in practice.

1 Show up. Show up does not mean merely arrive ready for anything. Show up with the appropriate attitude. Show up with the right posture. Show up, not just physically, but show up prepared. For me, showing up requires a tremendous amount of preparation. I cannot walk into the rehearsal room without having done months of intensive research, in-depth trial-and-error thinking and freewheeling around a given project. I show up prepared. But all of this preparation only earns me the right to enter the rehearsal hall. It gives me the permission to "show up." Once in the room, I have to let go of all of the preparation and I have to pay attention to what is happening.
2 Pay attention. How to pay attention to what is happening and not to what you want to happen? How to be attentive to the gap between your expectations and the reality of the moments unfolding in the

room? Paying attention demands energy and patience. Paying attention should cost you something. Directors often assume that their job is to arrive with all guns firing and then keep the barrage up until opening night. Perhaps this is not such an effective idea. "Do not be a motorboat. Be a sailboat," advised the director and theorist Richard Schechner. Behaving like a motorboat does not allow you to pay close attention and respond to the vicissitudes of the ongoing currents in rehearsal. "Actors will always provide plenty of useful hot air," said Schechner.

3 Tell the truth. In rehearsal, a director's primary job is to be the actors' first audience. Actors adjust their performances based upon the feedback that they receive from the director. Some directors offer feedback in the form of extensive notes and others give feedback simply in their responsiveness in the heat of the scene work. What matters is the director's physical, psychic and emotional connection to what happens, her taste and readiness to tell the truth.

The collaborative process requires from everyone the willingness to tell the truth and also the capacity to negotiate the feedback. The truth is not always expressed in words. A look of dismay or confusion can speak volumes. An audience in preview performances of a play can tell the truth about the production through their silence or nervousness or laughter. Based upon the truth that others offer, we can note the physical sensation that the observation triggers in our body, assess, renew the connection to our own taste and truth, and then adjust.

4 Don't be attached to the results. Strive hard for a result but do not be attached to it. What a paradox! How is it possible to be fully committed to the process but not personally attached to the results? Why is this paradox necessary? We work hard to achieve a successful outcome and we want the result to be good. We must be motivated and clear about our goals and about our strategies throughout the process. So why then must we not be attached to the result? To answer this question, it might help to cultivate the humility to understand that you do not own the fruits of your labor. Plus, if you attach yourself to premeditated results, you probably will not be able to see what is happening in front of you.

Getting stuck and getting unstuck

The human species is built for motion. Our bodies are engineered to move, to anticipate change and to adjust. But getting stuck happens. Getting stuck is part of the creative process, but ultimately it can also be destructive. Without strategy and cunning, it is easy to get bogged down. Initially the recent economic downturn brought us to our knees. We were forced to face, with great discomfort, our unwarranted blindness to the destructive machinations of the private sector. We had to acknowledge our own complicity for looking in the other direction while greed and reckless gambling wrecked the economy. Getting stuck brought us into a new awareness of the tensile global connections and our unmistakable interdependence upon others in other parts of the world. We were undeniably stuck for a while and now, hopefully, there is renewed movement and action and a deeper sense of the world's interconnectedness.

Getting stuck can be exceedingly productive. Wallowing in the mud of necessary confusion is part of the creative and innovative process. Sometimes standing still is the only way to move forwards. The discomfort of being stuck is a necessary step towards change, towards movement. Taking the pause to experience the state of stuck-ness can allow for the kind of spaciousness that stimulates new thoughts, images, directions and action.

But there is also the kind of stuck-ness that is not at all helpful.

Morgan Jenness, a dramaturg and an agent for playwrights, reads more plays per day than anyone I know. For the many years that I have known Morgan I have invariably found her carrying a hefty stack of scripts wherever she goes. Personally I find reading scripts, reading plays, very difficult. For me, plays are the most challenging literature to read because they demand an unparalleled investment of undivided attention and imagination. The words on the page are meant to inspire stage pictures and flights of associations. As opposed to performance theory, non-fiction or novels, the process of reading plays is challenging for me. I admire Morgan's prolific ability to read plays and I once asked her how she managed to ingest so many different scripts every single day. She told me that when she first opens a script, she reads very quickly. Whenever she senses a stop in the flow of the writing she turns over the top corner of the page and then continues on. Subsequently, when she meets with the playwright, she opens to the pages with the page corners turned over and asks why the flow of the play stops in that spot.

When Morgan told me about her process with plays and playwrights, I recognized the usefulness of her method and I wanted to apply the "turning down the corner of the page" technique to my own process of rehearsal and collaboration. Getting stuck in rehearsal can be devastating and unproductive. How often are rehearsals bogged down in too much talk or theory? The flow stops, and the process is hijacked. To "turn down the page," it is necessary for every member of a collaborative team to develop sensitivity to the internal (personal) and external (group) moments of stuck-ness. Develop the fine tensile awareness to know exactly when the flow stops. This sensitivity alerts you to when things start grinding to a stop in the collaborative process. As a director, when I sense that there is too much talk, I use Bertolt Brecht's "Show Me" technique. I ask the actors to show, to do, to demonstrate or to point to rather than to talk.

> Any action is better than no action at all.
>
> (Norman Vincent Peale, minister, author)

The most effective way for me to get unstuck is to move. Move anywhere, anyhow and in any direction. The movement changes my position, attitude and point of view in relation to the problem. From this new perspective I begin to identify the obstacles and recognize the patterns that bring about the stuck-ness. Next, I try to break the problems into small manageable segments and take small manageable steps. But first, I have to move, just move.

One summer, Yoshiko Chuma, the Japanese-American choreographer and director of the School for Hard Knocks, a dance company based in New York City, invited me to drop by her rehearsal in a town hall in Belfast, Maine. I walked into the spacious daylight-filled hall to find the dancers and actors of the School for Hard Knocks gathered onstage looking a bit confused. Yoshiko, who speaks English with a heavy Japanese accent despite her many years of living in New York, had suddenly shouted in their direction: "One, two, three, go! One, two, three, go!" The performers looked at her, confused, and asked: "What do you mean, Yoshiko? One, two, three, go what? Go where?" Again Yoshiko simply shouted, "One, two, three, go!" And then, without further discussion, the actors and dancers did indeed start to move across the wooden floor and their movement was expressive and soulful. And so the rehearsal continued and plenty of new material was generated. I was impressed and inwardly I decided to try out Yoshiko's "One, two, three, go!" technique in my own rehearsals.

About a year later I ran into Yoshiko back in New York City and I said, "Yoshiko, I use your 'One, two, three, go!' technique and it works very well." "Oh," responded Yoshiko impishly. "I don't say one, two, three anymore. I just say 'Go.'"

Collaboration with your own brain

> Imagination is more important than knowledge.
>
> (Albert Einstein, theoretical physicist)

Every play offers dramatically different experiences for actors, who, depending upon the specifics of their roles, radically alter their inner landscapes, change their frames of reference and shift their relationships to the world. Whether by imagining specific circumstances or by putting on special clothes and shoes that modify their sensation of movement or by executing precise actions that tap into radically diverse feelings, actors change perspective and they change their minds for each role they play.

Any artistic enterprise requires a change in perspective, literally a change in brain function. Creativity does not rely on a single brain region but rather many parts interact and collaborate in the cognitive processes. Innovation demands the ability to change one's mind with alacrity and dexterity. Different brain regions must be recruited to do different tasks, and they must work in concert, as a team, to get the job done. To move effectively from associative rumination to critical think-ing to intuitive action to objective judgment and so on is crucial to the process. Each phase of innovation requires completely different neuronal pathways and synaptic activity.

To illustrate how easily the brain can switch from one synaptic pathway to the next, try this: remember a nursery rhyme. Now say it out loud. In order to access the nursery rhyme, you changed brain functions. If someone had been watching you they probably would have noticed that your eyes traveled up and to the right before you could recite the rhyme. The body participates in each and every brain-state switch.

To collaborate successfully with your own brain, it helps to learn a little bit about how the brain functions. Neuroscience, a field that is presently exploding with insight and new discoveries, can help to explain the changes in brain function necessary to changing perspectives during the creative process. But creation and innovation do not happen in any prescribed order; rather, the brain switches constantly from one brain state to the next, altering the synaptic patterning from moment to moment.

Thanks to recent advances in the technology of fMRI neuroimaging machines, neuroscience has made great strides in understanding the alterations that happen in the brain during the creative state. The fMRI tracks the areas that literally "light up" as neurons fire in different parts of the brain during various brain functions. The research with fMRIs allows us to distinguish different brain states at work during the creative process. What is clear is that in order to collaborate with your own brain you need to be able to switch brain states effortlessly. Below are six brain states that are invaluable in the creative process.

Loosening critical thought

During the creative process it is necessary to go through a period of absorption where you allow yourself to let go of critical assessment in order to absorb information non-judgmentally. This is a very rich purposeful letting go, taking in the world around you and allowing the environs to work upon you. The key to this brain function is curiosity and fascination. During this process, your mind is open to new experiences and ideas and you delay judgment.

In this stage, intuition is key and it is necessary to bypass activity in the prefrontal cortex of the brain. Sometimes called the executive brain, the prefrontal cortex is the newest evolutionary addition to the brain and makes language, reasoning and planning possible. Less participation by the prefrontal cortex allows information, stimuli and associations to flood in, overcrowd and stimulate the brain without judgment or inhibition shutting out the stimuli.

At other phases in the development and implementation of a project, the special facilities of the executive brain are crucial.

Allowing for absorption and delayed judgment leads to what Marshall McLuhan, quoting International Business Machines (IBM), called "information overload equals pattern recognition." Inquisitiveness leads to this condition of non-judgmental, non-inhibited absorption. This is the brain function that leads me in the research process or allows me to notice daily life around me in a fresh and non-goal-oriented way.

I spend countless hours preparing to direct a production, studying themes, history and subjects around the play, voraciously reading and then flipping from one book to the next, meandering, making detours from the research and taking occasional naps. It is often upon waking from a nap that the disparate ideas converge into an inkling of how to approach the play. This ability to make connections demands a loosening of the power of critical thought and openness to the wide universe of stimuli rather than the tyranny of simplistic interpretation.

Thinking associatively

Another phase in the creative process requires the brain to think associatively and to make connections between disparate, divergent notions and ideas. You try to see the relationships between things without judgment. This brain function also bypasses the prefrontal cortex. Allow yourself to be consumed with interest. Open your mind to new experiences and ideas. Hope that thought does not shut options down into one solution, but rather opens up multiple possibilities. Thinking is infinite rather than finite and the act of juggling disparate ideas simultaneously is key. Be receptive to increased information coming in through the senses, both from the environment and from your internal terrain and memories. Take naps. Allow things outside of your usual dominion to attract your attention.

This process allows me to grasp connections between disparate ideas and notions. Rationality does not belong in this phase of the process because rationality's method closes options down into one solution. Later, in the editing stage, rationality is useful but if activated too early it can devastate the crucial phases of discovery and insight. Looking too soon and with desperation or impatience at these incongruent ideas from a rational brainset can be confusing because in this perspective nothing seems to make any sense. And yet this senselessness is vital in certain phases of the creative process.

Patterns and pictures

As work on a project continues, the brain switches to a metaphorical envisioning function, a theater of the mind where the imagination can play with and manipulate the surrounding world, can picture the fictional world and its landscapes.

This is a non-verbal realm where patterns and pictures emerge and the landscape is figurative rather than literal. Thinking in this way, it is imaginatively possible to turn a properly dressed lady on the street into a dangerous witch on a broomstick. Actors use envisioning thinking to imagine the circumstances of a character. Stanislavsky's "what if" requires this brain function, which allows us to endow familiar shapes or ideas with fictional properties.

Judgment and evaluation

After absorbing disparate ideas, making connections and envisioning, the time has come for judgment and evaluation. At this pivotal phase in the process, it becomes necessary to think critically, to choose and to discriminate from the myriad possibilities that are swimming around in the imagination and to decide what to keep, what to cut and how to proceed. Switch to a mind that discriminates and chooses. Trust your taste. Plan carefully and then make decisions with alacrity and certainty. This part of the process demands a completely different set of synaptic activities, a distinctive kind of thinking and a different cognitive network. The brain shifts into a mode that capitalizes upon its ability to evaluate, judge, make plans, discriminate, edit and cut. These decisions arise from the working memory of the brain: solving problems via purposeful planning, establishing goals, abstract reasoning and decision-making.

Playwright Charles Mee treats the world as if it were his library. He forages and appropriates what he finds fascinating from the world around him, often from artists and writers that he admires or from random bloggers on the internet, and then he assembles the wide-ranging material into a play. What makes the plays a product of his imagination and not simply a collection of other people's output? It is his judgment, his taste, his arrangement and his editing that make the plays uniquely his own.

Pains and triumphs as fuel

When your ego and your frustration intrudes with the "little me" brain function, use it. This brain function probably feels the most familiar to those of us brought up in secular consumerist cultures. This "little me" brain state can be mined for perseverance, diligence and will. We all have hopes and we have anxieties and this preoccupation with the self precipitates the "little me" brainset, the cognitive process in which obsession with personal triumphs, anguish, dissatisfaction and irritation reigns. And yet this is also a very useful brain function in the journey towards artistic expression or innovation of any kind.

I suspect that there is a relationship between mood and creativity. I am skeptical about overmedicating and aestheticizing natural mood swings because I know from personal experience that dissatisfaction is an important ingredient in the recipe of the creative act. The brain is able to transform personal anguish, worry, anxiety and irritation into useful expression. The dissatisfactions of living, the self-consciousness, the ego and the ego's vulnerabilities offer motivation to communicate, to formulate work. Our personal pains and triumphs become fuel for the will and perseverance necessary to bring our work out into the larger world. The "little me" thinking is useful for career decisions.

Moments of flow

When the flow finally happens, enjoy it. Ride it. Your hard work and digressions have paid off.

Watching pianist Keith Jarrett in concert is the clearest example I can think of to illustrate the "moments of flow" brain function in action. Jarrett is a composer and a performer who straddles the line between jazz and classical music. His live improvisations draw upon classical references, ethnic folk music, blues, gospel, jazz and his own compositional proclivities. In his performance I witnessed the fusion of a human being with the ebb and flow of his inspirations and influences. And it was all happening in the heat of the moment's improvisation fueled by a lifetime of practice.

Scientists have been having a tough time hooking up artists and scientists to fMRI machines in such moments of flow, but they can describe the activity in the brain: activation of the temporal lobe and the pre-motor areas, deactivation of the left prefrontal cortex and mild continuous activation of the reward center. In this brain state time disappears and one loses a sense of the self. The focus is totally on the task at hand. The artist becomes absorbed in and at one with the work. The sensation, the experience seems to be orchestrated by outside forces.

The key, the entryway into this brain state is practice. To experience flow, a great deal of experience in a chosen field is necessary. In his book *Outliers*, Malcolm Gladwell proposes that 10,000 hours of practice is needed before this brain state can be achieved. But this flow is precisely the pay-off for all of the practice undergone. When the pilot "Sully" Sullenberger successfully landed his US Airways plane in the Hudson River off Manhattan in 2009, and the 155 passengers and crew aboard the aircraft survived, his feat was attributed to the fact that he had flown for over 30 years. The correct brain function and flow seem to have kicked in at the right moment.

> Genius, in truth, means little more than the faculty of perceiving in an unhabitual way.
>
> (William James, philosopher and psychologist)

Thanks to the miraculous complexity of the human brain and with the help of new discoveries in neuroscience, each of us has the capacity to experience the world in radically different ways depending upon the brain function that we elect to use. Each of us is capable of perceiving the same event in significantly different ways depending upon how we position our priorities and how we use different brain functions or synaptic pathways.

Whether in collaboration with your own brain, collaborating with a group to mount a new play, collaborating over a long period of time with a fixed company or engaged in cross-disciplinary collaboration, the ground rules are similar. Collaboration requires generosity, openness, a sense of adventure, a love of active culture, tenacity, truth telling, interest in others, decisiveness and willingness, at any moment, to give up attachment to the final result.

Chapter 10

Politics

Art does not organize parties, nor is it the servant or colleague of power. Rather, the work of art becomes a political force simply through the faithful representation of the spirit. It is a political act to create an image of the self or of the collective.

(Lewis Hyde, essayist, cultural critic)

Could it be a mirage? At lunch with SITI Company colleagues at the edge of a rushing stream in the far reaches of a mountain range in a secluded part of Japan, we could see from the distance a tiny black dot moving in our direction. The vision gradually transformed into a solid line of black cars. As the cars slowly approached, I wondered who on earth might be in them.

Each summer, between 1992 and 1995, SITI Company spent a month in residence in Toga-mura, Japan to rehearse and premiere a new play. Toga is a remote village in the midst of rice fields between steep, wooded slopes where theater director Tadashi Suzuki presides over a theater compound and an international arts festival. To arrive in Toga-mura from anywhere requires a monumental journey. For us, the trip entailed a long plane ride from J. F. K. Airport in New York to Narita Airport in Tokyo, then a trek across the city to Tokyo's other airport to spend the night. The next morning the flight to the city of Toyama was followed by a long van ride, several hours up and up endless winding, narrow roads, along steep embankments and past glassy lakes into the mountainous area called the "Japanese Alps," finally arriving at our destination: the scenic village of Toga. The journey is exhausting and demanding. Once there, the silence and remoteness of the place crashes in upon the senses.

As the black cars approached from the distance – or *was* it a mirage? – I knew that wherever they were coming from, the journey must have been a very long one. Why had they come? What were they up to?

Suzuki initially chose the remote site of Toga-mura to distance his company from the hustle and bustle of urban areas and to forge a genre of theater that he believed could become essential and significant in Japan and internationally. Inspired by French director Jean-Louis Barrault's theater-house in Paris, the Gassho-style farmhouses were perfect for Suzuki's purposes. When he established the center in Toga in 1976, Suzuki's friends and colleagues were puzzled and intrigued. Why had he withdrawn to the distant mountains after launching a successful career in Tokyo? Toga was known historically as a place where Samurai warriors were banished. Why would he establish a theater center there? What for? At first, the Japanese theater world could not figure out what Suzuki was up to.

During his initial years in Toga-mura, living in the mountains was full of hardship and struggle. Money was tight. Suzuki and his company of actors and collaborators hired themselves out to work as day laborers for local reforestation and they did not shy away from the intense physical labor of cutting down trees in the mountains and constructing roads. Nevertheless, the SCOT Company (Suzuki Company of Toga) prevailed over the challenges to become what it is today. Over the years, with great perseverance and fortitude, Toga became a destination. Suzuki founded the Toga International Arts Festival in 1982, the very first truly international theater festival in Japan. With the remarkable and innovative architectural designs of Suzuki's close friend Arata Isozaki, the company transformed traditional Japanese farmhouses in Toga into functioning theaters and support buildings and constructed a 900-seat outdoor theater based upon the design of an ancient Greek theater, facing a pristine lake with the vista of hills in the distance. In these theaters Suzuki directed groundbreaking productions of reimagined classic plays. He then launched an international arts festival to which people from around the world eventually flocked each August, making the long, long journey from far away.

In the summer of 1995, Suzuki added a large new theater to the complex, again designed by the architect Isozaki. This was the very same summer that the line of black cars headed from the distance towards us.

On the day of the theater's official opening, Mrs. Ikuku Saito, Suzuki's executive director, asked me to suspend our afternoon rehearsal in order to attend the opening festivities for the new theater. I was happy to oblige. At lunch that day, sitting with my colleagues at the edge of the river that ran through Toga-mura, the vision appeared from the distance. It began as a dot on the horizon and then turned into a line of official black government cars moving slowly in our direction. As the cars passed by, solemn men in dark suits waved at us from the back of the cars. We waved back. The men seemed accustomed to waving at people on the sides of roads. The long line of cars moved past us and turned into the theater compound and up the hill towards the SCOT offices. And then it was clear to us that these important gentlemen had travelled to Toga for the opening ceremonies of the new theater. These busy dignitaries, government officials and heads of corporations made the long journey because they felt that being present would reflect well on them. They deemed it valuable to be present at the launch of Suzuki's newest venture and they saw his enterprise as a connector, uniting disparate parts of Japanese society.

Suzuki always puts on a good show and the opening ceremonies were no exception. Shinto priests conducted elaborate stomping and vocal ceremonies welcoming benevolent deities into the new theater. After many official speeches and toasts, the assembled enjoyed a delicious feast on the outdoor stage while the sun sank down behind the adjacent lake and mountains. But it was not only the show and the refreshments that brought these important dignitaries to Toga-mura.

Tadashi Suzuki approaches the theater as an art form that belongs in the public arena. He expects dignitaries as well as general audiences to be part of his enterprise. When I consider the relationship between artists and the public sphere in the United States, I sense that the connection has been corrupted. Artists have developed bad posture in relation to the world at large. Our shapes do not communicate power or strength. Our backs bend in humility as we pathetically extend a hand for donations.

Social systems within concentric circles

Starting around the time of the McCarthy era in the early 1950s, American artists lost touch with the vibrant role that they had heretofore played in society. The mass blacklisting and scaremongering of the time gave birth to a trope that I grew up hearing, "art and politics do not mix." Fearing the personal consequences of political engagement, several generations of American artists relinquished their connection to the political sphere and disengaged the link between political opinion and clear artistic expression. Artists developed the habit of kowtowing to hegemonic power.

Encouraged by Suzuki's sturdy relationship to the realm of politics and the economic system, I began to question my own assumptions about the place of American artists in the world. How do we situate ourselves? What does our posture express to the world at large? What response are we expecting from others and how do our expectations affect the way we speak about ourselves? Perhaps, I thought, we should not present ourselves, hat in hand, as show makers, but rather as culture shifters. Can we begin to think of ourselves, rather than stagers of plays, as orchestrators of social interactions in which a performance is a part, but only a fragment, of that interaction? Can we develop communities of individuals who are participants in an ongoing dialogue? Can we improve our posture and reassess the assumptions we hold about the relationship of our profession to the world?

At its best, the theater is a highly political enterprise. It is political not in the sense that we normally use the word, but political in the basic philosophic sense: a consideration of how human beings organize societies, not as unchangeable and part of the natural order, but rather as open to transformation. The theater is political in its interrogations: how do we arrange our collective life, our social practices, our patterns of family life, our economic systems and our political institutions?

In the United States, when the word *political* is joined with the word *theater*, what generally comes to mind are didactic productions about current events that use satire or agitprop to promote social change or to raise consciousness. But Tadashi Suzuki's theater is not political in a didactic sense. His productions, while often critical of the culture that supports them, are rarely about current events and do not directly try to change public policy. And yet his plays are both artistically and politically powerful. He places himself in the center of the polis, even from the distance of Toga-mura.

What distinguishes the theater from all other art forms is that the theater is the only art form that is *always* about social systems. Every play asks: Can we get along? Can we get along as a society? Can we get along in this room? How might we get along better?

Societies exist in concentric circles – the society of the audience, the society of the actors, the society of the actors and the audience together, the society of family, of town, of work, of country. A society is a group that thinks things through together. This explains why it is disappointing to attend the theater when few people show up. The experience of a theater is dependent upon who is in the room.

At its most democratic, the theater encourages us to face thorny issues together by examining our failures rather than our successes. As opposed to the commercial media that provide a pulpit to the loudest screamer, theater can give voice to those who are generally not heard and can permit discussion of that which is unspeakable. The Greek plays are brilliant conduits for thinking-things-through-together because they persist in asking crucial questions about family, war, sacrifice, hubris, karma and how we organize ourselves into societies. The theater offers us the practice of democracy in its ancient manifestation.

The origins of theater in the western world were rooted in the idea of a social experiment called democracy. The form of democracy that we inherited from the Greeks is vastly different from its starting point. But tracing democracy's trajectory can be instructive.

The invention of theater coincided with the foundations of democracy in Ancient Greece. In the sixth century BC, Athens was a city-state divided among four warring tribes troubled by chronic clan conflicts and tyrants. In 534 BC, frustrated by the clashes among his fellow citizens, Pistratus, an enlightened general who also founded the first Athenian library, initiated an annual theater festival in Athens. Until then theatrical events were mostly assorted choral shows, played throughout the city separately for the different tribes. At this new festival, all four opposing tribes came into a common space and shared a collective experience. The result was groundbreaking. Within a generation democracy was a reality. Euripides, Aeschylus and Sophocles were among the celebrated playwrights for this new kind of theater. This annual theater festival in Athens gave birth to a new democratic system and the fabric of Athenian consciousness altered completely. The city was then re-districted to reflect this democratic ideal of cooperation and thinking-things-through-together.

Thinking-things-through-together

Democracy and theater are inextricably linked. In Greece during the fifth century BC it was a requirement of citizenship to attend the theater. People came together as an entire society to sit in one place and recount the same stories to one another. The Greeks understood that it was not enough to put key domestic and political crimes on trial in a court of law, but it was also important for the population to consider the larger social questions that these events provoked. Theater-making and theater-going were attempts to find common ground, to come together and collectively consider, via metaphor and storytelling, issues that were very difficult to grasp in daily life. Greek plays and the performances of them were embodiments of the very tricky questions that the society was facing. The theater created the conditions for collective thinking-through.

Shared contemplation and pluralistic thinking can sever differences and also demonstrate how alike we actually are. In this way, we feel less separate and alone. The theater is the art form that can best create the

circumstances for the process of this collective thinking-through because
its essential nature is participatory.

Every production asks the audience to participate in the creation of
the performance in the very moment of its occurrence. The theater
audience learns from one another how to contribute to the collective
experience of the play. Their participation can be associative, physical,
imaginative, emotional or intellectual. The combined force of shared
spectatorship enriches the experience of the play for everyone present.

The way a group thinks together matters. A new idea borrowed from
economics called *collective intelligence* proposes that what determines
the inventiveness and rate of cultural change in a population is equivalent to the amount of meaningful interaction between individuals. The
theater in particular seems to be a forum in which people can think
things through *together*. We assemble in the context of the theater to
ask the following questions: What kind of life and social system have
we inherited? What are the myths that we have received? How are we
getting along as a society? How are we getting along in this room? How
might we get along better? Can we identify with the conflicts happening
on stage? Can I have empathy if I do not identify? Can I cultivate
empathy? Are there alternative actions that I can take in my life? The
theater exists to reflect upon and propose ways that humans might exist
together effectively. The theater is also a place of discourse, consciousness and plurality. The theater can create the circumstances where
audiences and actors coexist with differing points of view and find
some kind of unity within a pluralistic social situation.

But the thinking-things-through process is not instantaneous any
more than any experience is truly meaningful until it has been digested
and sorted out. The thinking-things-through process is an act of individual
and collective digestion that requires time, absorption and assimilation.
The current appetite for talkbacks or post-performance discussions in
theaters everywhere is a signal that audiences are hungry to share the
process of thinking-things-through-together with the artists.

Jaron Lanier, a cutting edge pioneer in virtual reality and new technologies, spoke at a recent conference and asked his audience not to
blog, text or tweet while he was speaking. "If you listen first, and write
later, then whatever you write will have had time to filter through your
brain, and you'll be *in* what you say. This is what makes you exist. If
you are only a reflector of information, are you really there?"

Theater is gossip and gossip is what all human beings, when there
is more than one of them, do. We love to talk about other people,
give our opinions of their merits or lack thereof, assess their character

and motives, learn about their activities and thoughts. We are social beings, curious about others, and a human universal is talking to others about others. Across the fence in the backyard, on the phone, in the restaurant, we offer tidbits of information and insights about the people we know and observe.

(Rocco Landesman, theater producer)

I like gossip. I enjoy knowing what people are doing and what is happening in the world around me. Perhaps my taste for gossip has something to do with the fact that, as neuroscientists point out, gossiping gives the body a dopamine spike. We get a little high on gossip.

The origin of gossip is linked to nitpicking and grooming in primates. Grooming has a stress-relieving effect because it is like a back rub, stimulating the production of dopamine, oxytocin and endorphins in the one being groomed. The action of grooming in primates is a hygienic and therapeutic practice, but also a crucial social activity, a device for creating, maintaining and repairing social bonds.

According to leading linguists and neuroscientists, spoken language originated in something like gossip. As early human groups grew larger and larger, the amount of grooming necessary to maintain a full array of social relations grew prohibitively complex and expensive. In order to survive and thrive, our prehistoric ancestors had to be in the know about the inner workings of their community. Who can you trust? Who can you hunt with? And thus was born spoken language. The tongue moved while air passed through the lungs.

Gossip continues to fulfill this function. Hearing things "through the grapevine" is necessary to figuring out how to negotiate the world. Information is passed from person to person in conversations like one finds in barbershops, supermarket lines and beauty parlors. Gossip in human societies plays exactly the same role as grooming does in primate societies.

Although gossip is an important social activity and helps to maintain transparency in social systems, it is completely different than thinking-things-through-together. The much slower process of comprehension, reflection and thinking-things-through often requires intense listening, physical discomfort and agonizing patience. The undigested noise of Facebook, texting and Twitter is a modern manifestation of gossip and an important hegemonic device to promote social transparency and visibility. But distinct from unprocessed gossip, thinking-things-through-together is vital to the development of a society.

Thanks to the internet, we have access to plenty of gossip and essentially anything that anyone would ever want to know. But we are so inundated with information that we do not have time to process it. Neal Gabler in an op-ed piece in *The New York Times* entitled "The Elusive Big Idea" described our present society as one that no longer thinks things through. He claims that as a culture we have substituted information for ideas, and he laments the time that we engaged in the development of ideas by thinking things through in order to comprehend them. "Great ideas," he wrote, "explain the world and one another to us." At its most democratic, the theater works on us and encourages us to face thorny issues together by examining our failures rather than our successes and it offers us the practice of democracy in its ancient manifestation.

The message and the messenger

> Metaphor, the artist's fundamental tool, is forgiving and generous. It is not held captive by fact or tribe or convention or politics. It suggests what might be possible and says, "You! In the audience, you can do this. You can look at things differently and do things differently. Blue can be orange!"
>
> (Anna Deavere Smith, actress, playwright)

The day before his first inauguration, Barak Obama visited a homeless shelter, removed his jacket, picked up a paint roller and was photographed for a short time helping to paint a wall. At one point, looking over his shoulder, he spoke with a reporter saying that this is what Americans need to do now: pitch in and help. The visual image of his action was both symbolic and expressive. The message was clear. His action was clear.

The philosopher Paul Woodruff defines theater as "The art by which human beings make or find human action worth watching in a measured time and place."

What was the message embedded in Obama's action? Paint roller in hand, was he offering us a return to authentic citizenry? Was he asking citizens to examine their own personal habits and passivity? Gore Vidal suggested that in the United States we were once considered citizens, and then we were transformed into consumers. With Obama's gesture had we arrived at a historical crossroads where we might transform from a passive culture to an active one?

An actor's job is to deliver the message with clarity through actions that are worth watching. Was Obama acting? Is an actor the messenger or the message?

During the course of a performance, theater audiences experience two plays simultaneously. On a conscious level the audience follows the fiction, the story written by the playwright and enacted by actors. But simultaneously, and often on an unconscious level, the audience experiences the event of a real community of real people enacting the play. In the embodiment of the fiction, the community of actors demonstrates, from one moment to the next, how well or badly their social system is working. No matter how dysfunctional the characters in the play, the community of actors who perform the play must operate at the height of their abilities. The enactment of a play demands generosity and cooperation between the individuals on the stage. Each actor receives and transmits stimuli, making split-second adjustments moment by moment by moment. When they are not able to function well together, the audience's experience is compromised.

The community of artists proposes, within the fabric of every production, nothing less than a model society. This is their message. The actors are the messengers.

The subject of the theater is, at its core, community. The story is not only the story of a fictional community within the dramatic context of the play, it is also the story of the actual communities that have assembled within the "measured time and place" set aside for the performance: the actors and the audience. These two real-time communities have gathered for the *rite* of enactment. A *rite* is the performance of a ritual and the theater contains vast amounts of ritual.

In 1922–3, the Moscow Art Theatre performed plays by Anton Chekhov and Maxim Gorky on tour throughout the United States. Young American audiences, galvanized by what they saw onstage, pursued the Russian actors and their director, Constantin Stanislavsky, wanting to study and to learn from them. I realize now that it was not only the new technique of acting that these young people were so excited about, but also the *way* that the actors inhabited the stage together. A visible demonstration of *how* people can coexist, the productions proposed nothing less than a new social dramaturgy: an alternative to the top-down hierarchy of star-led vehicles and melodramatic acting methods common in the United States at that time. There were no stars; the acting company was an ensemble. Their intense cooperation was palpable and real.

The early part of the twentieth century exploded in scientific, artistic and political upheaval. Albert Einstein's special relativity, Werner Heisenberg's uncertainty principle, Pablo Picasso's cubism, Ivan Pavlov's research about human conditioning, Sigmund Freud's discovery of the unconscious, Arnold Schoenberg's musical experiments and Sergei Eisenstein's film montages all demanded new methods and means for inhabiting the planet. The theater was uniquely capable of proposing the nuts and bolts of how new social systems could coexist and flourish in light of the new paradigms that these breakthroughs engendered. Stanislavsky and his collaborators found a way to integrate influences from developments in psychology, science, art and the social experiment of the Russian Revolution into the fabric of their theater. The Moscow Art Theatre was not only enacting plays by Chekhov and Gorky, but also suggesting alternate ways of being together in the world.

During the era of the war in Vietnam, the United States experienced the beginnings of a cultural revolution. Galvanized by the civil rights movement, the activities of the Students for a Democratic Society (SDS) and a fervor to end the war in Vietnam, young people challenged the status quo of the materialist post-World War II mentality, criticizing American society for its focus on career advancement and material possessions, its military strength and its racism. I was 18 years old in 1969 when I attended the three-day Woodstock Festival. Feeling a generational alliance to what seemed like a cultural revolution, I travelled with my friends in a beat-up VW van to the site where hundreds of thousands of people had gathered to listen to music and try out new ways of being with one another. The immense possibilities of peace and love left me breathless and hopeful. The way that people were acting together at the crowded festival seemed to embody a proposition about alternatives to the present social and political systems. The central idea of non-violence and communal hegemony was galvanizing to me. But the promise of a "Woodstock Nation" never fully materialized; rather, it was eventually coopted and trivialized.

The more recent Occupy movement began in a small square in downtown Manhattan near Wall Street. Its influence has spread globally to many different countries and cultures where people are gathering to contest the values and power of the ever expanding corporate culture. When I visited Zuccotti Park in Manhattan during the height of Occupy Wall Street (OWS), everyone in the packed tiny public space was engaged in serious conversations about the economy. The gathering felt familiar, reminding me of my experience at Woodstock as well as my work in the theater. The face-to-face interaction, the mutual cooperation and the acoustic nature of the experience of OWS are fundamental conditions of the theater.

In an op-ed piece in The New York Times, the architecture critic Michael Kimmelman considered the effect of place on the viral nature of the Occupy Wall Street movement. "We tend to underestimate the power of physical places," he wrote. He quoted one of the activists, who used the phrase "an architecture of consciousness." The close proximity within the OWS sphere provoked face-to-face conversations, and these conversations engendered nothing less than a global consciousness and dialogue about what went wrong within the capitalist system.

Before it was shut down, Zuccotti Park provided "an architecture of consciousness," an island of discourse where differing opinions and attitudes were allowed to coexist. The immediacy, the unmediated nature of the experience and the storytelling that felt so familiar to me, a theater person, suggested the necessity of unmediated environments. The participatory and collaborative interaction proposed nothing less than a new social system.

Aristotle believed that the human voice and face-to-face conversation were directly linked to civic order. The fact that the Occupiers were not allowed to use megaphones or amplifiers created the conditions for "mic checks." People were forced by circumstance to listen to one another and repeat each other's words. The nature of groups repeating the speaker's words, sentences, phrases and paragraphs is significant. The repetition of ideas forces the repeater to listen in a very particular way. Normally when one listens, the prefrontal cortex of the brain, often called the executive brain, responds rapidly in order to judge the incoming information, parsing out what to agree with and what to take issue with. The listening and responding at OWS allowed the words to temporarily bypass the prefrontal cortex and saturate other parts of the brain that are less immediately logical and judgmental. Listening is receiving. Perhaps the outlawing of amplification in Zuccotti Park was part of what created the very effective architecture of consciousness.

Revolutions in small rooms

In the case of Occupy Wall Street, social media like Facebook and Twitter brought people together and organized the events, but *nothing* could substitute for being present, together, united in time and space. Social media get you *to* the park but then what happens *in* the park is an entirely different matter. Immediacy is key. The unamplified voices, people telling stories, speaking from personal experience is crucial to the experience. Like OWS, the theater can create the circumstances where audiences and actors coexist with differing points of view and perhaps find a unity within a pluralistic social situation.

The current maelstrom of technological advances, innovations in communications, breakthroughs in physics, neuroscience, nanotechnology and digital media require concomitant innovation in systems of social interactions. We need to learn how to get along together all over again. The theater is uniquely positioned to re-evaluate the meaning of democracy and to figure out once again how humans can flourish in concert with one another.

In an op-ed piece in *The New York Times*, Rabbi Jonathan Sacks compared the Darwinian instinct for survival to the empathetic, community-minded impulse.

> We hand on our genes as individuals but we survive as members of groups, and groups can exist only when individuals act not solely for their own advantage but for the sake of the group as a whole.

In this consumerist, highly mediated culture, much of our life as individuals is spent struggling to survive. The survival instinct is compulsory and necessary. But amidst the jittery barrage of life in our over-stimulated environment, it is increasingly difficult to acquire focus, patience and restraint. What might provide the opportunity to steady and focus the senses? What might help us to negotiate our fidgety, edgy world with grace? How can we find space for reflection, contemplation and working-things-through?

In his piece Sacks proposes that religion exists to provide people with a way to slow down and join the realm of altruism and empathy. Historically, the theater originated in the realm of religion. Communities gathered together to consider their lives together in the light of the larger universe. I believe that this aspect of togetherness is shared with a theater audience as well.

Both art and theater are instruments that reassess the pattern of habitual reactions and find a sense of the eternal in the midst of the quickly accelerating present moment. Contemplation of art in a group, in a community, can help rejigger expectations, calm down the body and connect with both the past and those nearby. The art experience in the presence of others requires sharp attention, mutual respect, mental shifts, stillness, language skills and receptivity, which in turn can provoke rich shared experiences.

I feel and I act as an entirely different person depending upon momentary circumstances. When panicked, even in instances of day-to-day frustration like being placed on hold during a phone call or being the target of rude behavior at the supermarket, my response has the potential to be quick, impulsive and even violent. The ancient brain responds to primal prompts with fear and self-preservation. The vicious chemical cortisol shoots through my body. I do not think things through. Acting in self-interest, I can easily become an example of Darwinian survival mechanisms. I can be selfish and defensive, withdrawing and lashing out simultaneously. I can think of my own well-being and not care for the wellbeing of others. I can become self-protective, jealous and removed from others.

When overly concerned with our own survival or that of our progeny, we create boundaries between others and ourselves. But my atavistic self is also a lonely self. In my attempt at self-preservation, I attempt to control my environment. I try to stop the flow of change. I create boundaries. I grab at whatever pleasure is available and hold on for dear life. I want to win. I want to succeed.

These quick, emotive, instinctive individual responses are derived from the ancient parts of the brain, the fight or flight, the fear and protective mechanism. The strategies that help us to survive from one day to the next and ensure successful procreation and preservation are also the tactics that cause emotional pain.

On the other hand, the prefrontal cortex fosters consideration of others and the group. If I can slow down and access my altruistic nature, my experience of life will be completely different, less lonely, less egotistical and self-serving and more appreciative of those around me. This slowing down demands patience and purposeful restraint. In the midst of the unpleasant chemical rush of cortisol flowing throughout the body, I can try to recognize the impulse to act selfishly and self-protectively. Instead of lashing out, I can try to practice moderation and patience. The essence of civilization is restraint. Limiting one's freedom for the common good lies at the heart of growing from infancy into maturity.

In service of what?

In the midst of a SITI Company strategic planning committee meeting, Leon Ingulsrud, one of the three artistic directors of SITI Company, leaned over to me and quietly spoke the following words: "Anne, fifteen years ago, you said that you had about fifteen 'theatrical essays' in the form of plays to 'wright' with the company. And that's what we did; we followed your lead and constructed many productions based upon your fertile ideas. But what is your idea now, moving forward? What will we be doing for the next ten years?" At that moment Leon's question felt intrusive and aggressive. It upset my equilibrium. And I know that my equilibrium was upset because he was asking an important question that I needed to seriously consider.

Not long afterwards I read Simon Sinek's book entitled *Start with Why: How Great Leaders Inspire Everyone to Take Action*. Sinek distinguishes between leaders who start with *why* and those who start with *what*. The great innovators and entrepreneurs, he maintains, always start with the *why*. The *what* and the *how* are a result of the *why*. Individuals and communities who share the same *why* find the *what*, because of the *why*. People are drawn to others not because they love the *what*, but rather because they feel that they share the same *why*. I believe, for example, that people are drawn to the Occupy movement because of a shared *why*. People are drawn out of themselves for highly personal reasons. They are drawn out of themselves for themselves.

I had to ask myself, what is my *why* now and in service of what? I could feel the answer on the tip of my being but I could not as yet articulate it.

Soon afterwards, I attended a performance at the Brooklyn Academy of Music, a stunning display of virtuosity and theatricality that left me completely cold. I could not personally relate to the *why* of the production. I could feel no shared community onstage or in the audience and I sensed no community forged between stage and audience. All I could feel was the insinuation of one big controlling ego, the director. For me, this was a problem.

In contrast, the playwright and performer Taylor Mac's work seems deeply rooted in the *why*. He described his project about the history of popular music. Meant to take the form of a 24-hour concert, he was in the process of searching through music from the 1770s to the present decade in order to find 250 songs from 24 decades. I asked Taylor how he chooses the songs. "I am looking for songs that create community," he said. "Oh!" I exclaimed and asked Taylor what kinds of songs create community. "Some music tends to make the listener internal and contemplative," he said, "and other music connects people."

Perhaps Taylor Mac's work is successful with audiences because he is deeply connected to the *why* of his enterprise. His mission to find songs that create community and connect people is a vital one for our present climate.

> I see there's something going on in civilization, which is coming with great vehemence at us.
>
> (Werner Herzog, filmmaker)

In the autumn of 1989 the Berlin Wall fell and in a momentary suspension in the onslaught of events anything was possible. It was not a given that Eastern Europe would choose capitalism as the inevitable next system upon which it would build its future. Although vast international corporate interests were ready to pounce and profit from the regime change, for just a few moments, as young people stood expectantly atop the crumbling walls, the once communist countries might have chosen an alternative to unbridled capitalism. Ultimately the crunch and pressure of all the forces conspiring towards unrestrained capitalism won the day.

I believe that we are at such a critical turning point right now. The market free fall and the revelation that vast wealth had been built on bad debt and false promises, the rampant escalation in unemployment and the ever widening disparity in wealth suggest that the time is ripe to ask what is important and to choose values, ethics and desires that can lead us forward. What do we wish for? How might things be different?

Jeanette Winterson wrote in *The Times* about the role of art during a recession. She suggested that art would continue to do what it always does, "asking us to rename what is important." In the crush of cultural decomposition we can attempt to describe new paradigms, alternate values and goals. In the crisis of collapse, if we can find the necessary psychic spaciousness, we have the opportunity to look around, reflect upon the situation and rename what is important. This renaming is the start, the beginning.

After Leon's challenging question about what SITI Company will do and what we will make in the coming years, I had to ask myself once again: what are we doing and *why*? After 20 years of working together, SITI Company is a finely trained ensemble of like-minded artists. But, in service of *what*?

In conversation with the composer Julia Wolfe, I suddenly fully grasped my current *why*. She had just proposed that SITI Company collaborate with the Bang on a Can All Stars, her new-music ensemble, to stage a music-theater version of her oratorio *Steel Hammer*. Every fiber of my being shouted "yes." My excitement and the feeling of rightness about the project was not simply because I like Julia Wolfe's music, but also because the prospect of two strong communities from different artistic disciplines collaborating to make something new felt so right to me. What interests me now is how the community of SITI Company can intersect with other communities to make new model societies. My *why* celebrates cross-disciplinary collaboration.

SITI's recent alliances with the Martha Graham Dance Company to make *American Document*, a re-imagining of a 1938 piece by Martha Graham, and with the Bill T. Jones/Arnie Zane Dance Company for *A Rite*, a piece about Igor Stravinsky's *Rite of Spring*, are part of this new direction. The encounters between SITI Company and two world-class dance companies became the subliminal subject matter of the productions.

The role of the audience

Artists in some societies are given a "grace note" – a kind of compass – that inspires them to suggest, imagine and suppose. The successful ones conjure up a desired or fictional reality before that reality exists. People like to believe in possibility. That must be one of our primal drives. If the artist's narrative is intoxicating enough, it will cause audiences to engage in actions that change the world.

(Anna Deavere Smith, actress, playwright)

In 1987, the actor Henry Stram performed the role of Cusins in a production of George Bernard Shaw's play *Major Barbara* at Baltimore Center Stage. Towards the end of the rather long and windy third act during a sleepy Sunday matinee, Henry made a critical mistake. His character had an important plot-point line about his parentage and his appropriateness to take over the Undershaft Munitions Works. In describing why he should be entitled to run the foundry, Henry misspoke a line from the play and rather than saying "My mother is my father's deceased wife's sister; and in this island I am consequently a foundling!" he said instead, "My father is my brother's deceased wife's sister; and in this island I am consequently a foundling." To his immense surprise, the entire audience, who Henry had until that moment supposed was a typical sleepy matinee crowd, gasped loudly, as one, at his slip. And Henry at that moment realized that audiences *do* in fact listen, that what we say on the stage really does register.

The potential for a powerful communal experience in the act of coming together is a constant incentive for going to the theater. Unlike film and television, theater is unfinished until the audience completes the equation. When you enter the theater nothing is guaranteed; you do not really know what is going to happen. How you watch and what you are doing while you watch will have an impact on what is happening on the stage. Within a very short time, minutes into the *rite* of any performance, actors generally sense what kind of audience they are dealing with and adjust accordingly.

The director William Ball in his seminal book entitled *A Sense of Direction* wrote that he considers an audience heroic because it spends the hours gathered in the theater *not* thinking about itself. Depending upon the circumstances and the atmosphere, being in a group can make us smarter or dumber. This fact can work for the benefit or to the detriment of any performance because performers are highly dependent upon the mood and receptive capabilities of the community gathered to receive it. The audience teaches itself how to experience a production and the intelligence of a group arises within the time set aside for the performance. In the collaboration of attention, audience members have the potential to engender nothing less than a rapture of mutual interest. But in opening ourselves to other people, we take the risk that the experience may be disappointing. An unsuccessful gathering can render confusion and disorientation. And there is always doubt present because the story that is embodied isn't actually happening. It *is* fiction. The audience's reading of a performance is actually an act of interpretation. The ambiguity generated by the simultaneous believing and non-believing creates a certain critical distance that Antonin Artaud called *the theater and its double*. But ultimately, the theater gives us the tools to measure our own lives against what we see depicted on stage.

Chapter 11

Sustenance

Great works of art pass through us like storm winds, flinging open the
doors of perception, pressing upon the architecture of our beliefs with
their transformative powers. We seek to record their impact, to convey to
others the quality and force of the experience. We would persuade them to
lay themselves open to it.

(George Steiner, literary critic, essayist)

I am a tapestry woven from borrowed bits and pieces of the thousands
of influencers, famous and unknown, most of whom I have never met. I
am a copycat. I voluntarily and involuntarily, sometimes automatically,
incorporate discrete behavior-fragments of other people into my personal repertoire. I am only half joking when I say that Gertrude Stein is
my mother and that Bertolt Brecht is my father. Everything that I do
and think, even writing here, seems to be modified and borrowed from
others. But innovation results from re-combining things. If I have any
artistic integrity it is because I apply my own taste to organizing the
influences into a montage that feels pleasing to me.

Even though I have often been described as an "avant garde" theater
director, I am rarely concerned about making anything new; rather, I
am deeply invested in studying the past, in studying history. I feel that a
large part of my job in the theater is to give voice to dead people
who still have something to say. The poet W. H. Auden described the
artist's job as communication with the dead. If I listen closely enough I
hear voices.

Musician John Mellencamp speaking with Terry Gross on public
radio's *Fresh Air* proposed that whatever he heard or experienced belon-
ged to him. He said that all input is fodder for his songs and that he has
no qualms about incorporating anything he encounters into his art.

Artists and inventors rarely create something out of nothing, but rather
use the components that already exist in the environment to make new

things. The world is a grocery store and the artist's job is to eat the world. What is eaten, or experienced, can be transformed into sustenance, ideas, energy and action. But for this transformation to occur, it is necessary to be open enough to be stimulated by one's surroundings and sensitive enough to be altered by what is encountered there.

T. S. Eliot, in his seminal 1919 essay "Tradition and the Individual Talent," proposed that the notion that artists are supposed to be original is actually a fairly recent idea. Historically, interest in an artist was based upon what she or he created from the remnants of inherited culture. I am relieved by Eliot's proposal. As contemporary artists, we are all members of the largest collective of all, the dead. The dead are present as the living past and they survive in our literature, art and through the words of those who speak about them. New work is expressed through the digestion and re-assembly of the alphabet of the old.

According to Eliot, the artist's "historical sense" allows him or her to function as a conduit for the past. The mind is a poetic archive, a "receptacle" for storing "feelings, phrases, images" which "remain there" until combined to form a new compound. The experience of language yields more language. The experience of art yields more art.

We are debris arrangers. Equipped with what we have inherited, we try to make a life, make a living and make art. We are assemblers. We forge received parts into meaningful compositions. This state of affairs is our plight and our destiny, but it also offers the opportunity to find meaning as well as to find communion with others.

> Take something. Change it. Change it again.
>
> (Jasper Johns, visual artist)

The composer Philip Glass's father owned an auto mechanic shop in Baltimore. Working on people's cars eventually led him to fix car radios. Finally he got rid of the cars and opened a store that sold and repaired radios. This led him to buy a music store where he sold records. As a young boy, Philip Glass worked in his father's music store. One of Glass's jobs was to break faulty LPs that had been returned by customers in order to ship the pieces back to the manufacturer in boxes. I imagine him in the basement of the shop, jumping up and down on damaged records. Perhaps some aspects of the music that Glass has composed since then reflect his experience of jumping up and down on records. We make hay from the fields we tread.

The notion of an isolated genius forging a new world in private is erroneous. I am even suspicious of the idea of sole ownership. Innovation is made possible by the width and breadth of a person's rummaging around the world, in traffic with the living and the dead. It is by transgressing the boundaries that separate us that we begin to find solutions to the world's present complexities because inclusion and incorporation of "the other" creates the conditions for innovation. The concept of exclusivity and segregation is essentially anti-creative. Cultivating our fields with influences that are beyond our own immediate understanding allows for the necessary irritation and consequent cross-fertilization that leads to invention.

Steven Johnson in a book entitled *Where Good Ideas Come From: The Natural History of Innovation* presents the notion of the "adjacent possible," which defines the preconditions for invention. He writes, "The adjacent possible is a kind of shadow future, hovering on the edges of the present state of things, a map of all the ways in which the present can reinvent itself." What hovers on the edges are components that already exist in the environment. We innovate precisely based upon what our predecessors, either natural or human, forged from *their* environment. In 1440 Johannes Gutenberg developed the first printing press from the technology of a screw-type wine press from the Rhine Valley. This technology remained standard until the twentieth century. Right now, as always, innovators and artists are creating the adjacent possible for future generations.

Here I present six little personal snapshot stories about Virginia Woolf, Martha Graham, Pina Bausch, Merce Cunningham, Robert Wilson and Charles L. Mee, Jr. In each story I try to capture one way that each artist has provided me with nourishment and sustenance. Because I have eaten at their tables, I carry them in my body. Some are living and some are dead, but all are part of me.

Virginia Woolf

An artist recreates history, not like a historian, but as a poet. The artist takes the communal ideas and associations that surround the various gods of his or her time and plays with them, inventing another story for these mythic characters.

(Robert Wilson, theater director)

At first we stand in the shadows of giants, possibly in awe, then we attempt to knock them down and perhaps even kill them. As time passes, we recognize their role in our lives and we finally offer them the heartfelt thanks that they deserve for being so present for us. It is in this spirit that I approached Virginia Woolf and the play *Room*. I seem to have passed through all of these stages in the proximity of her example.

Virginia Woolf stands steadily before me as a mountain or as what she described in *Moments of Being* as a rod:

> If I were painting myself I should have to find some – rod, shall I say – something that would stand for the conception. It proves that one's life is not confined to one's body and what one says and does; one is living all the time in relation to certain background rods or conceptions.

I often make plays about people I admire, people who have been a "rod" for me. I feel that the work on these plays is a way to eat them and then stand firmly upon their shoulders. I ingest their lives and they become part of me. I have made plays about Orson Welles, Gertrude Stein, Marshall McLuhan, Robert Wilson, Leonard Bernstein and about Virginia Woolf.

In 2000, after a very painful breakup, I bought a house in upstate New York. My friends all thought of this abrupt act on my part as an extreme sort of retail therapy and they all worried about me. But to me, buying the house was not only the fulfillment of a long-term dream, but also a creative act of survival during an emotionally difficult period. The large house, built around 1850 and in great need of renovation, included a big brown boxy barn on the property. During the summer following the final sale and before launching renovation, I lived in the empty rooms of the house and wrote the bulk of my first book of essays, *A Director Prepares*; also, along with SITI Company actress Ellen Lauren, we brought *Room* into existence.

A great inspiration to me since I was first able to read her novels, diaries and essays, Virginia Woolf played a huge role in my development. As a teenager, reading *To the Lighthouse* was transformative. At the time I described the feeling of reading, "It's not a book. It is an experience." I distinctly remember the sensation of being lifted up through the tension of the writing and then suddenly, unexpectedly, released midair to fly free fall. With the play *Room* I wanted to create this experience for an audience.

Room was to become the second of a triptych of one-person plays: *bob*, *Room* and *Score*. Following the formula of the genesis of the play *bob*, a solo piece based on the art of the theater director Robert Wilson, and later *Score*, based upon the conductor and composer Leonard Bernstein, I spent a great deal of time reading the source material, in this case Woolf, collecting snippets and paragraphs that directly addressed my own nagging personal question: how can one live creatively in the face of all the difficulties, setbacks and irritations of daily life? The text originated from Woolf's essays and lectures as well as her final novel, *Between the Acts*. I mailed 150 pages of text to writer and dramaturg Jocelyn Clarke in Dublin. Several months later he sent back a beautiful 30-page script, *Room*. Ellen read the play out loud in its entirety in the front room of my house and then she proceeded to learn it by heart.

To begin we established a few simple rules. Each day I chose a room in the house where I waited. Ellen would find me, enter and speak as much of the text as she could. Then she would leave the room. After a few minutes I would follow and meet her in another part of the house to discuss what we had both learned.

Ellen and I, both accustomed to years in crowded rehearsal halls with stage managers, other actors, producers, dramaturgs, designers and onlookers present, decided to begin together, just the two of us, at home. Literally. Ellen owns a farmhouse a few minutes' walk from mine. To get from her red house to mine is a short walk across a small bridge over a creek. We decided to rehearse in a special way and in a private manner. Each day, at the appointed hour, Ellen walked across the creek to my house and looked for me while I waited for her in one of the rooms. She would enter the room and begin speaking to me from the beginning of the play.

Good evening.
Before I begin, I must ask you to imagine a room.
Any room. But it must be your room.
A room of which you are mistress, and where you close the door to the world outside, and sit and think; perhaps even write.
A retreat.
A sanctuary.
A refuge.
Call it what you will. But it must be a room that you can call your own.
Do you have such a room?
I pity you if you do not.
A room of one's own is not a luxury but a necessity.
This is not a pretty room, is it? Some of the furniture, well, I have seen better. But it will do.
It is our room now.
How are your seats? Comfortable?
Good.

And so on until she reached the end of the text that she had managed to memorize by that day. The process was intimate. One woman, Ellen

Lauren, spoke the words of another woman from the beginning of the previous century, Virginia Woolf, to yet another woman, me, who sat waiting for her in a room in a house. Ellen spoke to me personally, in a way that I might understand and that might open up the myriad meanings of the text rather than closing it down to one interpretation. Each day, as she memorized more of the play, our sessions lengthened.

As the pages of memorized text expanded, we began to change the rules. One day, for example, Ellen would arrive and lead me down to the creek and speak to me there. Another day she would lead me through a field where we would pick wild flowers as she spoke and while I listened. She would usually look directly at me to see if I was still with her, following her journey of thought and words.

Once Ellen could speak the entire text, we began to rehearse the staging in the cleared upstairs loft in my barn. The only object we found in that space was a low wooden red chair with arms. This chair became the single object in our eventual set design. Ultimately a new and more polished chair was found for the production, but the influence of that small red chair has always remained, and it continues to sit in the corner of my dining room. During the rehearsals in the barn, the only sound design for *Room* was the shriek of birds, an occasional plane passing over, the wind or the rain.

By the end of the summer, back in New York City and moving towards the scheduled premiere of *Room* at the Wexner Center for the Arts in Columbus, Ohio, the time came, of course, to bring the stage manager, designers and fellow company members into our room. For the initial rehearsal, both Ellen and I were filled with excitement but also with trepidation and nervousness to share our very intimate process with our colleagues. By force of luck we could not find a rehearsal hall to rent on that day so I offered my apartment on the Upper West Side. Ellen stood in the empty dining room while the rest of us, including sound designer Darron West, crammed into the little living room looking through the open threshold of a pair of double doors. Ellen stood in the bare room with only a mantlepiece behind her upon which sat my family's old Tiffany clock. It just so happened that as she was about to speak the opening lines, the clock sounded the hour. Darron jumped up and shouted, "I'm in!" The sound of a clock striking the hour became the central sound and metaphor for the production. And with that, we had begun the next phase of the production *Room,* which has toured extensively now for well over a decade, sharing the vision of Virginia Woolf.

Martha Graham

> Existence is no more than the precarious attainment of relevance in an
> intensely mobile flux of past, present and future.
>
> (Susan Sontag, writer)

In 2010, Janet Eilber, the current artistic director of the Martha Graham
Dance Company, invited me to re-imagine a 1938 Graham piece entitled
American Document to present as part of their New York season.
Honored that I was considered for the assignment, I agreed immedi-
ately. Graham had had an enormous impact upon me and influenced
how I think about acting, directing and performance. Through film
footage of her dances, photos, interviews and an engaging and
informative biography by Agnes de Mille, I had been shaped by
Graham's example long before I experienced any of her dances firsthand.
Singlehandedly Graham created a new paradigm in dance and linked
the modernist movement with theater. I often wonder if Constantin
Stanislavsky had not visited the United States in 1922, affecting generations of actors and actor training, would it have been Martha Graham
who would have taught the American theater how to act?

The new creation of *American Document* became a remarkable
collaboration between the dancers of the Martha Graham Dance
Company and the actors and designers of SITI Company. To conceive a
new iteration of *American Document* required us to engage in real conversation with Graham's legacy. We started by studying photographs and
brief film excerpts of the piece as well as written descriptions and
Graham's own handwritten choreographic notes about the original
production.

When Martha Graham made *American Document*, she was falling in
love with a young dancer, Erick Hawkins, whom she later married.
Much to her female dancers' consternation, Graham placed Hawkins at
the center of the piece as well as at the center of the company. *American
Document* was to be the first Graham dance to include men and spoken
text: Erick Hawkins and the actor who played the character of the
"interlocutor" who spoke the text. The piece was a success and it
toured widely until 1944.

To begin the process of rehearsing *American Document* (2010), the
two companies agreed to reciprocate teaching their respective trainings.
The Martha Graham dancers learned Suzuki and Viewpoints. The SITI
actors studied the Martha Graham technique. Sharing the respective
trainings was both disturbing and transformative for everyone. The
SITI Company actors, older than the dancers, toiled with the specifics

and mechanics of Graham's technique. The dancers struggled to move in a way that simultaneously allowed them to speak. In our daily work on *American Document*, the actors and the dancers were challenged but they also seemed to be touching upon deeply embedded similarities. The basic principles of the shared training felt familiar to both groups. Janet Eilber, who had worked intimately with Martha Graham, participated in the Suzuki training and afterwards she looked at me and said simply, "It's the same."

Perhaps in the more difficult moments of confronting novelty and exchange, it is helpful to remember Slovenian philosopher Slavoj Žižek's proposition that every true encounter is a form of harassment.

Ultimately what our forebears offer is permission. Martha Graham's commitment and the risks that she took in her lifetime give me the permission to be and to act differently than what had been acceptable before her. Graham allows me to approach the theater as a dramatic art form that articulates powerful emotionality through the expression of the body. By studying her and respecting her, by listening to what she had to say, I felt that I could begin to approach *American Document* and learn from her example.

Pina Bausch

> We are all curious collages, weird little planetoids that grow by accreting other people's habits and ideas and styles and tics and jokes and phrases and tunes and hopes and fears as if they were meteorites that came soaring out of the blue, collided with us, and stuck.
>
> (Douglas Hofstadter, cognitive scientist)

My first direct encounter with Pina Bausch happened in a circus tent in Munich, Germany in 1983 at a public dress rehearsal for her new piece *Nelken* (Carnations). I attended with both trepidation and skepticism. Based upon photos, books and firsthand accounts, she already exerted a profound influence on me even though I had never seen her work live. I had mined what I could for my own purposes from these secondary sources. Bausch's example proposed radical notions to me about physical drama and theatrical expressions of sexuality and intimacy. These ideas were useful in my own work as a director in the theater. My friends had accused me countless times of stealing from Bausch but I protested that I had never seen any of her pieces, only photographs of her work in books.

The tent was crowded and I ended up sitting under a scaffold. Pina Bausch herself sat above me watching and smoking. Throughout the run-through I observed her bony hand clenching a cigarette, steadily moving in spirals. I admit that I arrived in the tent for the dress rehearsal feeling already jaded and dubious about what I was about to encounter. "There is nothing that this company can do that will surprise me," I thought. "There is nothing that I do not already expect or know about." Meanwhile, in the midst of my preconceived notions about what was going to happen, I noticed that some of the dancers had arrived with armchairs and, one at a time, placed them on the stage, which was like a circus ring. Then, to my surprise, a woman dancer, after depositing a chair, waded into the audience, approached a male audience member, whispered in his ear, took his hand and then together they walked across the stage and out through the tent's entrance. Next, a male dancer invited a female spectator in a similar way and they walked out of the theater together. And then another and another audience member was escorted across the stage and out into the night, leaving a few empty seats behind like holes in the crowd. Meanwhile, a tall, slender dancer, Lutz Forster, walked to the center of the circus ring and began to sign to the tune of a scratchy version of Sophie Tucker singing "The Man I Love." All of a sudden, the lights abruptly leapt on, to reveal Lutz Forster standing in a massive field of pink and white carnations. "Damn it!" I shouted silently, "She got me."

Merce Cunningham

> When Francis Bacon approaches a white canvas its empty surface is already filled with the whole history of painting up to that moment, it is a compaction of all the clichés of representation already extant in the painter's world, in the painter's head, in the probability of what can be done on this surface.
>
> (Anne Carson, poet)

My experience of Merce Cunningham's work initially arrived through my body. Valda Setterfield, a glamorous Cunningham dancer, taught at Bard College where I was an undergraduate in the early 1970s. In those days I attended many dance classes and I rarely missed one of hers. I was actually a terrible dancer but I enjoyed the challenge of the elusive Cunningham technique. I think that Valda liked me, even though I was not a dancer, because I threw myself into whatever she put before us and I moved like a messy centrifugal force with gusto and optimism. At one point she stopped a class, pointed at me and said to the dancers, "Anne cannot dance, but she can move." When I graduated from Bard College and moved to Manhattan, I continued to take dance classes around the city and one of my destinations was the Merce Cunningham Studio on the top floor of Westbeth, a vast artists' community next to the Hudson River in the West Village. Cunningham and his company taught classes that my body never really understood. I always took my place in the back of the class and tried to follow but the logic never came easily to me. But what did become clear as I met dancers, artists and choreographers around the city was what a touchstone for everyone Cunningham had become. His innovations were so radical that really nothing has been the same ever since. He continually tried out new ways of combining disparate elements, elusive imagery, new technologies and chance elements into a single work. His collaborations with musicians and visual artists raised the bar on what was possible in exchange between art forms. His creative collaborations with John Cage affect the way that we speak to one another in SITI Company rehearsals to this day. "Let's Cage/Cunningham that moment," someone might say, meaning let's make two discrete moments and then put them together and see what comes of putting two ideas that seemingly have nothing to do with one another together. This is, of course, how Cage and Cunningham typically worked. The dancers heard the music, wore the costumes and saw the set for the first time on opening night. The coincidences that occur working in this manner are nothing short of a miraculous lesson in humility around the subject of artistic control.

Robert Wilson

> Wilson treats history not as a body of fact but a landscape of experiences. An anthology of images, of texts: knowledge as database. A menu. Food for thought.
>
> (Bonnie Marranca, critic, publisher)

As a director I define myself in relation to other theater artists who have thrown down the gauntlet via their productions. Robert Wilson is one of the figures in the world that stands as a rod, an orientation, a marker or a buoy in the ocean defining the parameters of recently crossed boundaries and newly explored waters.

Before I experienced any of Wilson's productions directly, I was already in a certain thrall to his legend. Even in the days before the internet, news traveled fast and I was captivated by countless stories about Wilson's monolithic vision and the adventures that his productions engendered both in audiences and in those who worked with him. The stories piqued a vicious curiosity in me. I regretted missing his early seminal works in New York, including *The Life and Times of Sigmund Freud* and *The Life and Times of Joseph Stalin*, the sprawling creations that stretched out through entire nights at Brooklyn Academy of Music. I knew about the avalanche of fascination that his *Deafman Glance* triggered in what seemed like the entire country of France. In Iran his seven-day spectacle entitled *KA MOUNTAIN AND GUARDenia Terrace* unfolded across a mountain range and was renowned in theater circles. By the time I arrived in New York City in 1974, fresh out of college and ready to begin a career as a theater director, Wilson already cast a long shadow.

My own direct experience with Wilson's work began with *A Letter to Queen Victoria* and soon afterwards *The $ Value of Man* and *Emily Likes the TV*. The rare ecospheres and atmospheres produced by these productions felt novel, strange and fascinating and I could not figure out what arrangement of sensibilities could create such enchantments. Around that time, in the mid to late 1970s, Wilson's loft on Spring Street, the Byrd Hoffman School for Byrds, attracted artists every Thursday evening when the doors opened and the world was invited in to join the "Byrds" in what seemed like elaborate rites and rituals. In 1976 at New York's Westbeth Center I sat in on a rehearsal showing of *Einstein on the Beach* during its gestation period. All of these occasions provoked my curiosity even further. But Robert Wilson the man remained an enigma. I went so far as to secretly follow him on the streets of New York City to try to figure out who he could possibly be, looking to see if he would cross some boundary that would reveal something about him that had not been evident to my eyes before.

Since those heady New York days I have kept track of Wilson's productions and the ups and downs of his career throughout Europe, Asia and the United States. I saw many segments of *the CIVIL warS: a tree is best measured when it is down*, Wilson's sprawling multi-national project before it was tragically shut/cut down shortly before hundreds of theater artists from around the world were to gather in Los Angeles to perform this massive work in its entirety for the Cultural Olympics of 1984.

Occasionally his work infuriated me. After seeing a production that felt overly formal or too cool, in despair I would think, "Oh, Bob has finally lost his Midas touch. He directs too many plays in too many places and now the passion, the life force is nowhere to be found."

In the spring of 1987, during one of my periods of impatience with Wilson's work, I was directing a play in West Berlin and attended his production of *Death, Destruction & Detroit II* at the Schaubühne. Even though I was ready to reject his work, I was also inextricably pulled towards it, but I went with no expectation of the delight and surprise that awaited me. I walked into the lavish theater building on the Kurfürstendamm, in which I had seen many productions and with which I was quite familiar, and I was immediately utterly disoriented by the spatial arrangement. Wilson had changed everything. He placed the audience upon swivel stools. Four stages filled all four sides of the theater. You could spin yourself around on the stools by holding on to metal railings designed specifically for the audience members to be able to do exactly that. And the performances were wonderful: funny, vaudevillian, tragic and with a distinct glow of mischief from each actor.

After the performance I went for a drink with the wonderful Schaubühne actor, Gerd Wameling, who had played a large role in *Death, Destruction & Detroit II*. "How did that miracle happen?" I asked Gerd. "How did the company and Bob pull that off? What an amazing production!" Gerd explained that the production came together over a rather long period of time. Wilson would fly in from La Scala or from Japan or from wherever in the world he was making plays, and he was usually quite exhausted. The actors pushed him. He pushed back. Somehow what they created together seemed to me to thrust theater, as I knew it, out of the twentieth century and into the twenty-first. Here I was, ready to dismiss him. Again and again he proved me wrong. Again and again he rocked my world when I least expected it.

Until then I had assumed that when you reach a state of exhaustion, you must take a break until the creative life and force returns. Gerd's story and my experience of *Death, Destruction & Detroit II* provoked a new insight into the whole issue of exhaustion and its role in creative development. Wilson's example showed me that through exhaustion it is possible to be catapulted into the next octave, to catch the next wave.

I learned from Wilson that when exhausted, when my guard is down, when I am no longer able to control the events around me with my own assumptions and preconceptions, things start to happen that are larger than the perimeters that I have predetermined. Within the exhaustion I have to be patient and to get out of my own way. And despite the exhaustion I have to stand vigilant to my preconceptions and assumptions and be ready to let them go. I have to make careful plans, create a schedule and then just "show up." Show up and be present. Tell the truth. Do not hold on to expectations of the outcome. Stuff happens. I just have to be patient, stay present and remain open to the unexpected.

Charles L. Mee, Jr.

I don't want to discover something new but something forgotten.

(Jerzy Grotowski, theater director and theorist)

Playwright Charles L. Mee, Jr. excavates the world to scavenge for bits and pieces that delight him. He organizes these bits and pieces into the content of his many adventurous plays. He was once an historian and occasionally uses the word "pillage" to describe how he appropriates history for his own plays. I once asked him, "Then what makes it a Charles Mee play?" He answered easily, "My taste." His taste organizes the bits of "pillaged" material and "wrights" it into a whole that is unique and original.

With Mee's permission, I pillaged his scripts, sampling freely from all of them, in order to compose yet another new play, which became *Café Variations*, a new SITI Company production. In addition to the plays, and very much in the spirit of Mee, we also scavenged through YouTube clips of Apache dances from the early part of the twentieth century, Edward Hopper paintings, old romantic movies and the catalogue of George and Ira Gershwin.

Café Variations is a great example of Mee's arms-wide-open-to-the-world attitude. The play is much larger than any single person involved in its genesis. I imagined that *Café Variations* would happen in the metaphorical arena of a café of my dreams. I am not a fan of Starbucks, which I consider to be an anti-café. I always felt cheated that I had never had the opportunity to experience the cafés of the Enlightenment or the cafés of Paris and Vienna during the latter part of the nineteenth century in which so many political and artistic movements fermented. These cafés seemed to be a living embodiment of pluralism. In them, revolutions were incited. Conversations that happened there changed entire social systems. I was intrigued by the idea of the café as an alternative context, a third realm, separate from the realm of the home or the realm of work and commerce. With *Café Variations* I wanted to create, through the fictional dreaming of theater, the café as a realm of public intercourse. I imagined our café as a magnet that has the power to draw people out of their homes, out of themselves and towards one another in an arena that is both public and social and yet one in which privacy is also possible. I wanted to create a café that instills the audience with a desire for such a place to exist.

But ultimately, in my description of the café of my dreams, am I not describing what I hope theater itself can be? The theater that I hope for is overflowing with voices from the past, set into patterns and stories that are recognizable and useful to those in the present; a theater that is fueled by politics; a theater sustained by the heat of deep practice; a theater that celebrates human error and tempts limits; a theater that offers journeys into the landscape of memory; a theater full of *kairos*; a theater that provokes empathy, that arrests time and in which opposition can flourish; a theater that proposes model communities within a collaborative environment; a theater that tells good stories about itself and others.